YOU, THE FINANCIAL MANAGER

RANNOI SEDUMO

YOU, THE FINANCIAL MANAGER

A JOURNEY TO PERSONAL FINANCIAL WELLNESS

INSPIRED PUBLISHING

You, the Financial Manager:

A Journey to Personal Financial Wellness

First Edition, First Imprint 2025
ISBN: 978-1-997467-18-2

Editor: Eloise Scoble

Published by: Inspired Publishing
PO Box 82058 | Southdale | 2135 Johannesburg, South Africa
info@inspiredpublishing.co.za | www.inspiredpublishing.co.za

Acknowledgements

This book would never have come to life without the support, inspiration, and encouragement of some very special people.

First and foremost, my deepest thanks go to my wife. Your love, patience, and understanding have meant everything to me. You carried so much of the load while I poured my heart into this project. Thank you for the time you sacrificed, for your quiet encouragement, and for always believing in what I was trying to build. Every late night and early morning was made possible because of your faith in me. I am forever grateful to you.

To Mr Mcedisi Vilakazi, my colleague and friend from my years in the Gauteng Provincial Government, thank you for planting the seed that started it all. I still remember our conversation about life after public service. When I said I wanted to retire at sixty, you told me, "Please dedicate some of your time in retirement to writing about civil service." Those words stayed with me. While this book is not about my time in government, that conversation stirred something in me that helped shape my purpose and direction.

And to everyone who, in quiet conversations or simple words of encouragement, reminded me that what I was teaching about money mattered, thank you. Your belief in this message gave me the courage to keep going when it felt difficult or slow.

This book carries pieces of each of you. Thank you for walking this journey with me.

Prologue
The Mirror and the Map

"Financial freedom is not a number. It's a feeling of peace when your values and your money finally align."

Those words capture the heart of this book. Before you open a spreadsheet, download an app, or calculate a single figure, pause for a moment.

Take a breath.

This book is not just about money. It is about you.

It is about the quiet decisions you make every day - the ones that shape your future more than you realise. It is about the weight you feel when bills pile up, the relief when things finally balance, and the pride that comes when you save a little more than you did last month. It is about the dreams that keep you awake at night, the ones you hold close but haven't yet dared to fund.

You may not think of yourself as a financial manager, but if you have ever earned, spent, saved, or worried about money, you already are one. Managing money is not reserved for experts in suits or people with financial degrees. It is for anyone who wants to live with a little more peace and a little less fear.

As Chris Brogan once said, "The goal is not more money. The goal is living life on your terms."

That is the true purpose of this journey. It is not about chasing wealth or counting coins—it is about creating a life that feels whole and aligned. Financial wellness is not a number in your bank account; it is a state of being. It is the clarity you feel when you finally understand where your money is going. It is the control that comes when you make choices based on values, not pressure. It is the confidence that grows when you believe you can build the life you want. And it is the capacity to respond with calm and wisdom when life takes an unexpected turn.

This book is your mirror and your map. It will help you see where you are now and guide you toward where you want to be. Along the way, you will learn to manage your money with intention, align it with your priorities, and build a life marked by purpose, peace, and possibility.

You do not need to be perfect to begin. You only need to be willing.

TABLE OF CONTENTS

CHAPTER 1

What Is Financial Wellness?

Money is one of those subjects that touches every part of our lives, yet it is also one of the most misunderstood. For some, the very thought of finances brings a knot to the stomach; for others, it is a source of pride or comparison. The truth is, money is not just about numbers. It is about peace, security, and how we live each day.

Financial wellness is the point where money supports your life rather than controls it. Imagine waking up each morning without that heavy cloud of worry about bills, loans, or uncertainty. Instead, you carry a quiet confidence; you know what you earn, what you owe and what you are working toward. More importantly, you know that your money decisions align with your deeper values.

As one writer put it, *"Wealth consists not in having great possessions, but in having few wants"* (Epictetus). Financial wellness is not about chasing more, but about finding balance, clarity, and direction. It's about having enough margin to breathe, to plan, and to live with purpose.

Think of financial wellness the way you think of health. Just as a healthy body allows you to walk, run, and enjoy life, financial wellness allows you to dream, to give, and to step into opportunities without being shackled by constant anxiety. Another saying goes, *"Do not save what is left after spending, but spend what is left after saving"* (Warren Buffett). Wisdom like this reminds us that the way we handle money is not just about today; it shapes tomorrow.

Most importantly, financial wellness is not a one-time achievement but a journey. Like tending a garden, it requires attention, patience, and care. You will have seasons of growth and seasons of challenge, but with steady commitment, it becomes a way of life that brings stability and freedom.

Financial wellness is a state of being, and like any state, it can **be measured, improved,** and **maintained.** We will unpack each of these as we go along.

Wellness Is Personal, But Not Vague

Financial wellness is not a one-size-fits-all picture. Just as physical health looks different for a marathon runner compared to a retiree, financial health also takes on different shapes depending on your season of life. A young graduate starting their first job has needs and goals that differ greatly from a parent raising three children, or from a small business owner preparing for retirement. What matters is not that your journey looks the same as someone else's, but that your financial life supports you where you are and helps you move toward where you want to be.

Despite these differences, there are **universal principles** that make up the foundation of financial wellness. Think of them as the vital signs of your financial life; markers you can check and strengthen over time:

- **Clarity**: You understand your financial situation and can see it clearly.

This means means being able to see your financial life without fog or confusion. It's knowing what comes in, what goes out, and what you're working toward. Many people avoid looking too closely at their money out of fear; fear of what they might find, or fear of facing past mistakes. But clarity is not about shame; it's about vision. Without it, you're walking in the dark, stumbling over the same obstacles again and again. With it, you can chart a path forward. As the writer James Clear reminds us, *"You do not rise to the level of your goals. You fall to the level of your systems."* Clarity is the first step in building a system that supports your goals.

- **Control**: You manage your money with intention rather than letting it drift.

Once you can see clearly, the next step is control. Control is not about rigid restriction; it's about intention. It's the difference between your money slipping through your fingers without notice and your money moving purposefully in the direction of your values. When you're in control, you spend, save, and invest with awareness rather than impulse. As the saying goes, *"The best way to predict your future is to create it."* Control is the daily practice of creating that future one decision at a time.

- **Confidence**: You feel secure about your financial future, not constantly second-guessing yourself.

Confidence flows naturally when clarity and control are in place. It doesn't mean you'll never worry, but it does mean you can face the future with calm assurance. Confidence is the sense that no matter what comes, an unexpected bill, a job change or even a global crisis, you are not defenceless. You have put systems in place, built habits of discipline, and learned to trust your own ability to respond. The poet Ralph Waldo Emerson once wrote, *"Self-trust is the first secret of success."* Financial confidence is self-trust in action: the knowledge that you are prepared to handle what life brings.

- **Capacity**: You have the ability to weather financial shocks and still pursue opportunities when they come.

Finally, wellness gives you capacity, the margin to breathe, to dream, and to respond when opportunities or challenges arise. Without capacity, even small setbacks feel overwhelming. With it, you have space to absorb shocks, adapt quickly, and even take risks that could lead to growth. Capacity is what allows you to move beyond survival into purpose. The author Stephen Covey put it simply: *"The key is not to prioritise what's on your schedule, but to schedule your priorities."* Building capacity means arranging your financial life so that your priorities such as family, growth, generosity and peace can thrive without being constantly squeezed out.

Together, these four principles of clarity, control, confidence and capacity form the framework of financial wellness. They are not about perfection but about progress. They give you both stability for today and strength for tomorrow.

The philosopher Seneca once wrote, *"Wealth is the slave of a wise man, the master of a fool."* Wellness, then, is not about how much you have, but how you relate to what you have. If you live with clarity, control, confidence, and capacity, money becomes a tool that serves you – rather than a master that controls you.

The Myth of the Financial Expert

It's easy to believe that money is best left to the professionals such as bankers in their glass offices, accountants with their spreadsheets, or economists speaking in complicated terms. But here's the truth: **if you earn, spend, save, or plan, you are a financial manager.**

You may not wear a suit or carry a calculator, but every single decision you make has financial weight. Buying groceries, deciding where to live, choosing whether to take on a new job, or even setting aside money for a rainy day are all acts of financial management. You are making choices every day that shape your future, whether or not you realise it.

This book is not about turning you into an economist. It is about helping you step into the role you already occupy with more clarity and confidence. As management thinker Peter Drucker once said, *"The best way to predict the future is to create it."* By learning to manage your finances consciously, you are creating a future where money supports your values, rather than controls them. Every person who engages in economic activity has the **capacity and responsibility** to manage their finances.

The myth of the "financial expert" says freedom is reserved for those with advanced degrees or insider knowledge. But the reality is that freedom comes from awareness, discipline, and intentional choices. Every person who participates in the flow of daily life, whether working, spending, giving or saving, has both the capacity and the responsibility to manage their money wisely.

This book is here to guide you on that journey: not with jargon or theories, but with practical steps and reflections that will help you become a **conscious, capable steward** of your financial life.

Why Measurement Matters

If wellness is a state, then it must be **observable**. You can't improve what you don't measure. Imagine trying to get fitter without ever stepping on a scale, noticing how your clothes fit or checking your energy levels; you'd have no way of knowing whether your efforts were making a difference. The same principle applies to financial wellness.

That's why this book introduces simple tools to help you assess where you stand financially, regardless of your income level, family size or life stage. These tools aren't about comparison or judgment; they're about clarity. Numbers, when used wisely, can shine a light on patterns and help you make better choices.

Some of the key markers you'll learn to track include:

- Your **net worth** - the difference between what you own and what you owe.
- Your **savings rate** - how much you're setting aside compared to what you earn.
- Your **debt-to-income ratio** - the portion of your income that goes to repayments.

- Your **financial resilience** - how prepared you are for life's unexpected expenses.

These aren't just abstract figures. They are **indicators of your financial health**, much like blood pressure or cholesterol readings are for your physical health.

They show you what's strong, what needs attention, and where you might be at risk.

As author James Clear puts it, *"You do not rise to the level of your goals, you fall to the level of your systems."* By paying attention to these measurements, you are building systems that keep your financial life steady and growing, no matter the season.

The Journey Ahead

In the chapters that follow, we'll walk step by step through the building blocks of financial wellness. Together, we'll look at how to **set goals that reflect what matters most to you,** how to **create a budget that brings order without adding stress**, how **to save and invest in ways that feel sustainable**, and how to **manage debt with wisdom rather than fear.** We'll also explore how to **protect the progress you make** through planning that gives you peace of mind.

Most importantly, you'll discover how to keep measuring and adjusting as life changes. Because life does change, with new jobs, new responsibilities, unexpected challenges and unexpected blessings. Financial wellness isn't a fixed destination; it's a journey that adapts as you grow.

Whether you're just starting your career, raising a family, or preparing for retirement, this book is for you. It's not about becoming rich; it's about becoming well. Financial wellness is not a finish line; it's a way of living with clarity, confidence, and resilience.

So let's begin. You are the manager of your financial life, and you already have what it takes to grow in wisdom and strength. The journey to wellness starts now.

As the author Henry David Thoreau once said, *"Wealth is the ability to fully experience life."* This is your opportunity to step into that kind of wealth, one decision, one habit, one step at a time.

REFLECTION QUESTIONS

What Is Financial Wellness?

- What does financial wellness mean to me personally?
- Do I feel in control of my money, or does it control me?
- Which part of my financial life brings me the most peace? Which part brings the most stress?
- What habits could I start today to grow in clarity and confidence?
- How might my values shape the way I set financial goals for the future?

WORKSHEET 1

Financial Wellness Indicators

Define what financial wellness means to you across four core indicators.

Indicator	Current Reality	Desired State	Actions to Improve
Clarity			
Control			
Confidence			
Capacity			

CHAPTER 2

Everyone Is a Financial Manager

If you've ever earned money, bought something, saved a little, or even worried about how to pay a bill, you've already stepped into the role of financial manager. You may not have called it that, but the truth is simple: anyone who handles money in any way is managing it.

If Chapter 1 showed us that financial wellness is about clarity, control, and confidence, then Chapter 2 reveals the role we all play: manager. The difference is that not all managers are alike. Some manage well, others poorly. Some take charge with intention; others drift along and let money manage them.

The real question is not *if* you are a financial manager, but *how well* you are managing.

Some people manage reactively, always putting out fires, paying bills late, or letting money slip away without noticing. Others manage cautiously, saving but perhaps too rigidly, missing opportunities to grow. And then there are those who manage with intention, planning, tracking, and making money serve their goals rather than control them.

Your management style is not fixed. It's shaped by habits, upbringing, and the beliefs you carry about money. Perhaps you grew up in a home where money was scarce, so now every decision is marked by fear. Or maybe you saw money wasted, and now you cling to it tightly. Recognising your current style is the first step toward improving it.

As Peter Drucker once said, *"What gets measured, gets managed."* The way you manage today determines the options you will have tomorrow. This chapter will help you reflect not on whether you are a financial manager, because you already are, but on what kind of one you are and how you can grow into a better one.

The Invisible Role We All Play

Think of it like running a household, a small business, or even a farm. Every person has income (the harvest), expenses (what it costs to live), debts (what is owed), and assets (what is owned). Whether you acknowledge it or not, you're sitting in the manager's chair. The difference lies in whether you're actively steering, or just reacting.

Some people avoid money decisions until crisis hits. Others spend without thinking, hoping things will work out. Some save diligently but never invest in opportunities. Others plan and adapt, balancing needs and future goals. These are all management styles, whether recognised or not.

Financial Styles We Fall Into

- **The Avoider**: ignores money issues, hoping they'll go away, only to face greater stress later.
- **The Spender**: enjoys life in the moment but often sacrifices long-term stability.
- **The Saver**: cautious and disciplined, but sometimes too fearful to take healthy risks.
- **The Planner**: balances today's needs with tomorrow's vision, using money as a tool.

Where do you see yourself in these patterns? You might notice you're a mix of more than one. Recognising your tendencies is the first step to leading yourself more wisely.

From Accidental to Intentional

The real shift comes when you stop being an *accidental* manager and start being an *intentional* one. That means every choice, whether it's buying groceries, taking out a loan or setting aside savings, is made with awareness and purpose. Intentional managers don't wait for money to dictate terms; they give money a clear assignment.

Like a business manager assigns every employee a role, so must you assign every pound or rand. Otherwise, idle money leaks away, and unmanaged debt grows silently.

Why This Mindset Matters

When you begin to see yourself as a financial manager, something shifts deep inside. Money is no longer just a source of stress or a mystery you hope will sort itself out. Instead, you begin to realise that you have a role, a voice, and a measure of control in how your financial story unfolds.

This shift changes how you relate to money in everyday life:

- **You stop feeling helpless and start feeling empowered.** Instead of thinking, *"I'll never get ahead"* or *"I'm just bad with money,"* you start saying, *"I can learn, I can plan, I can grow."* It's not about having all the answers, but about believing you are capable of leading yourself financially.
- **You stop avoiding financial conversations and start engaging with them.** Talking about money is often uncomfortable, whether with a partner, family or even with yourself. But when you embrace your role as manager, you approach these conversations with curiosity instead of fear. You ask questions, you seek advice, and you begin to make choices with clarity.
- **You stop drifting and start planning.** Drifting feels like living on autopilot, waiting for the next paycheque and reacting to whatever comes. Planning, on the other hand, means giving your money direction. You decide what matters most, you set priorities, and you build a path forward.

This mindset shift is not about achieving perfection or never making mistakes. It's about **ownership**. Ownership says: *"This is my life, my responsibility, and I will take charge with the tools and knowledge available to me."*

As James Clear, author of *Atomic Habits*, reminds us: *"Every action you take is a vote for the type of person you wish to become."* Each small decision, whether to save, spend or ignore, is shaping not only your financial outcome but also your identity as a steward of what you've been given.

The journey to financial wellness doesn't begin with money itself; it begins with how you see yourself in relation to it. Once you adopt the mindset of a manager, you move from passivity to purpose. You stop being someone money happens to, and you become someone who makes money serve your goals and values.

The Personal Financial Dashboard

Imagine trying to drive a car with no dashboard. You wouldn't know your speed, your fuel level, or whether the engine was about to overheat. You might get down the road for a while, but eventually you'd either break down or risk serious damage.

In the same way, your financial life needs a dashboard. It gives you a clear picture of where you are and helps you make better decisions as you move forward. Without it, you're driving blind. With it, you can adjust your course, slow down when needed, and accelerate when the road ahead is clear.

1. **Income** - This is the money flowing in from your work, side projects, or investments. It's the fuel for your financial journey.
2. **Expenses** - This is what flows out each month. Some expenses are fixed, like rent or mortgage, while others are variable, like eating out or entertainment. Tracking these helps you see where your money is really going.

3. **Savings** - This is the margin you set aside for emergencies, future goals, or long-term investments. Savings aren't just numbers in an account; they represent stability, opportunity, and peace of mind.

4. **Debt** - This is what you owe. Debt isn't just about repayment; it's about understanding how much of your future income is already spoken for and making a plan to free yourself from it.

5. **Net Worth** - This is the bigger picture: what you own minus what you owe. It's like the health check of your financial life, showing whether you are moving forward or sliding backward.

6. **Goals** - These are the destinations on your journey: saving for a home, paying off debt, building an emergency fund, or investing for the future. Without goals, the dashboard loses its purpose.

You don't need expensive software or complex systems to build your dashboard. A simple notebook, a budgeting app, or even a basic spreadsheet can do the job. The important thing is to begin. You need to **start tracking.**

The very act of writing things down begins to shift your awareness. When you track your spending, you begin to see patterns you may have ignored, such as the daily coffee that quietly adds up to hundreds a month, or the subscriptions that no longer serve you but still drain your account. Tracking brings what is hidden into the light, and once you see clearly, you can act wisely.

Starting small is better than waiting for the "perfect system." Even jotting down your income and expenses on paper each week builds awareness and creates accountability. Over time, those little notes become a story of your progress, showing you how far you've come, where you've stumbled and where you're gaining strength.

Think of tracking like taking your financial pulse. At first, it may feel awkward or unnecessary, but soon it becomes a natural rhythm of self-checking. And just as a doctor can't treat what isn't measured, you cannot improve what you refuse to track. The sooner you start, the sooner you begin moving from uncertainty to clarity.

As Benjamin Franklin wisely put it, *"An investment in knowledge pays the best interest."* Creating your financial dashboard is an act of knowledge. It gives you insight, clarity and the ability to make wise choices that serve your future.

The Manager's Responsibilities

When you accept that you are the manager of your own financial life, you also embrace certain responsibilities. These are not meant to weigh you down, but to empower you. They are the tools that help you shape your future instead of being shaped by circumstances.

Planning is where it begins. Just as an architect would never start building without a blueprint, you cannot expect financial stability without a plan. Setting goals and creating a budget give direction to your money so it works for you, not against you.

Monitoring is about paying attention. A good manager doesn't simply make a plan and walk away; they check in. By keeping track of your income, expenses, and savings, you can see whether you're on course or drifting off track.

Adjusting is the skill of flexibility. Life changes: jobs shift, families grow, emergencies happen. A wise financial manager responds to those changes by adapting the plan rather than abandoning it.

Learning keeps you growing. Just as technology or medicine evolves, so does the way we handle money. Reading, asking questions, and building your financial knowledge mean you're always better equipped to make sound decisions.

Think about it like this: a parent managing household bills might plan carefully each month, but when the electricity bill suddenly rises, they monitor their spending, adjust by cutting back on a few non-essentials, and perhaps even learn a new way to save energy going forward. That cycle of planning, monitoring, adjusting and learning is the quiet rhythm of wise financial management.

These are not burdens to dread but opportunities to embrace. They place the steering wheel firmly in your hands, reminding you that financial freedom isn't accidental – it's managed.

From Survival to Strategy

For many people, money management is about getting through the month. It's about making sure the rent is paid, the lights stay on, and food is on the table. That kind of survival thinking is real, and for a season it may even be necessary. But financial wellness invites us to move beyond **survival into strategy.**

When you begin to think strategically, money shifts from being a source of constant stress to becoming a tool that supports your goals. Instead of reacting to every bill and crisis, you start planning for the bigger picture. Your decisions are no longer about just the next meal or the next payment, but about shaping a future that reflects your values and hopes.

This book is designed to help you make that shift. You'll discover how to build your own financial dashboard, set goals that actually mean something to you, and manage your money with clarity and confidence. The aim isn't just balance sheets and budgets; it's a life where money supports you instead of controlling you.

So take a moment and speak this truth over yourself: **"I am the financial manager of my life."**

Let it sink in. It's not only a statement; it's a starting point. A declaration that you are no longer just surviving, but learning to manage your money with purpose and strategy.

REFLECTION QUESTIONS

Everyone Is a Financial Manager

- Do I see myself as the financial manager of my life? Why or why not?
- In what ways have I already been managing money, even without realising it?
- Where do I feel most confident in my financial decisions, and where do I feel uncertain?
- How might my mindset shift if I began to see money choices as opportunities rather than pressures?
- What small step can I take this week to manage my finances with more intention?

WORKSHEET 2

Personal Financial Dashboard

Capture a snapshot of your financial life.

Category	Current Amount	Notes / Actions
Income		
Expenses		
Savings		
Debt		
Net Worth		
Short-Term Goals		
Long-Term Goals		

CHAPTER 3

The Five Pillars of Financial Wellness

Financial wellness may look different for each of us, but the foundation that holds it steady is the same. Just as a house cannot stand without solid supports, your financial life rests on five essential pillars. These pillars help you build stability, adapt to change, and stand firm when life delivers the unexpected.

Think of them as the cornerstones of your money journey. If even one is weak or ignored, the whole structure feels shaky. But when all five are strengthened, you create balance, and balance brings peace.

As the saying goes, *"A house built on sand cannot withstand the storm, but a house built on rock stands firm."* In the same way, these five pillars give your financial life something unshakable to stand on. Let's take a closer look at each one.

1. Income Management: The Flow In

Your income is the fuel for your financial engine. It's what keeps the system moving, whether it comes from your salary, freelance work, a side hustle or passive streams like investments or rental property. Managing this flow in is the very first step toward wellness.

Key principles:

- **Know your total monthly income (after tax):** Awareness is the first step. Many people only think in gross salary terms, but what matters is what reaches your bank account. Break it down clearly so you know exactly what's available to work with.
- **Diversify your income sources where possible:** Relying on one stream of income can be risky. Even small side hustles or passive earnings create stability and options. Think of it as adding multiple rivers to feed your reservoir.
- **Understand your earning potential and how to grow it:** Your income doesn't have to stay static. Learning new skills, asking for a raise, or pursuing better opportunities can all expand your earning power.

Why it matters:

Without clarity about your income, it's easy to overspend or under-save. Many people live as though their earnings have no limits, only to find themselves stretched thin. Income is not just about what you bring in; it's about what you use wisely. When you learn to manage the flow in, you lay the groundwork for managing the flow out.

Once you know what flows in, the next step is learning how to manage what flows out.

2. Expense Control: The Flow Out

If income is the river flowing in, expenses are the stream flowing out. No matter how wide the river, if the outflow is uncontrolled, the reservoir soon runs dry. Expenses cover everything from the essentials such as rent, groceries and transport to the extras we choose, like entertainment, subscriptions or luxury treats.

Key principles:

- **Track your spending regularly:** Write it down, check your statements, or use an app. Tracking turns vague feelings into clear data. You'll spot leaks you didn't realise were draining you.
- **Differentiate between needs and wants:** Needs keep you alive and stable (food, housing, healthcare). Wants make life enjoyable but should not dominate your budget. Learning this balance is a discipline of freedom.
- **Avoid lifestyle inflation:** Just because your income increases doesn't mean your spending should rise at the same pace. Hold back, and channel the increase toward savings or investments instead of new liabilities.

Why it matters:

Unchecked spending is one of the fastest ways to financial stress. When you take control of your outflow, you create space to breathe, save, and invest. Expense control isn't about depriving yourself; it's about choosing balance and freedom.

As the old proverb goes, *"Beware of little expenses. A small leak will sink a great ship."* Keeping an eye on the small leaks helps you protect the bigger journey. Learning to master spending protects your future.

With income and expenses under control, you can turn your focus to the future, building stability and growth through savings and investment.

3. Savings and Investment: Building the Future

If expense control helps you stay afloat, savings and investment are the sails that carry you forward. Saving is about security; it cushions you against life's sudden storms. Investing is about growth; it allows your money to work for you, building something bigger over time. Together, they create stability and momentum.

Key principles:

- **Pay yourself first – save before you spend:** Treat savings like a fixed expense that must be paid, just like rent or electricity. When you prioritise it at the start of the month, you protect it from being swallowed by day-to-day spending.
- **Build an emergency fund (3–6 months of expenses):** Life is unpredictable. Having this buffer prevents small crises from becoming financial disasters.
- **Start investing early, even in small amounts:** The power of compounding means the earlier you start, the greater the effect. Even small amounts, invested consistently, grow into significant results over time.

Why it matters:

Without savings, even small setbacks can feel overwhelming. With savings, you have peace of mind. Investments, meanwhile, open the door to bigger goals like buying a home, supporting children's education, or retiring with dignity. They shift you from surviving today to preparing for tomorrow.

Albert Einstein famously called compound interest *"the eighth wonder of the world. He who understands it, earns it; he who doesn't, pays it."* Saving and investing wisely ensures you're on the right side of that equation.

But as you grow your wealth, it's vital to recognise the risks and responsibilities that come with it, and to manage debt wisely.

4. Risk and Debt Management: Guarding the Foundation

Risk is part of life. Illness, job loss or an unexpected accident can disrupt even the best financial plan. Debt, too, can either be a tool or a trap depending on how it's managed. To build true financial wellness, we must not only grow wealth but also guard against what can erode it.

Key principles:

- **Understand your debt - interest rates, terms, and total cost:** Write down what you owe, to whom, and at what cost. Seeing it clearly helps you prioritise repayment.
- **Avoid high-interest debt and unnecessary borrowing:** Not all debt is equal. A mortgage may build equity, but credit card debt can trap you. Choose carefully.
- **Use insurance to protect against major risks:** Health issues, accidents, or job loss can quickly erode financial stability. Insurance creates a safety net for both you and your family.
- **Build resilience through financial buffers and wise choices:** Living slightly below your means creates margin. Margin

becomes resilience. It's about building enough room so life's shocks don't collapse your foundation.

Why it matters:

Debt can undo years of progress if left unchecked, while unmanaged risks can wipe out savings overnight. Managing risk and debt is not about living in fear; it's about being prepared, steady and wise. As Benjamin Franklin once said, *"An ounce of prevention is worth a pound of cure."*

Once your foundation is guarded, the final step is to look ahead with wisdom and intentionality, protecting your progress and planning for the future.

5. Protection and Planning: Safeguarding the Journey

Financial wellness is not only about surviving today; it's about building tomorrow. Protection and planning give your financial journey structure, ensuring that what you build lasts and blesses others too.

Key principles:

- **Create a will and estate plan to protect your loved ones:** Without one, your assets may not be distributed according to your wishes. A will is not just legal; it's love in written form.
- **Plan for retirement early; time is your greatest ally:** Retirement planning isn't only for the elderly. The earlier you start, the lighter the burden later.
- **Review and update your financial documents regularly:** Life changes with marriage, children and job shifts. Your plans should reflect your current reality.

- **Align your plan with your values, not just your numbers:** Money can shape generations. Make sure what you build reflects what you believe. That's how wealth becomes legacy.

Why it matters:

Without protection and long-term planning, your financial progress can fade with time. But with them, you create peace of mind today and security for the future. Or as Seneca wisely put it, *"Luck is what happens when preparation meets opportunity."*

Bringing It All Together

Think of these pillars as the legs of a table. If one is weak or missing, the whole structure becomes unstable. Financial wellness is not about **perfection; it's about balance.**

You may find that one pillar feels strong while another needs attention. Perhaps your income is steady, but expenses are slipping out of control. Or maybe you're saving well but neglecting long-term planning. That's normal. The goal is not to master everything at once, but to steadily strengthen each area so your financial life can stand firm, even when tested.

A simple way to picture this is to imagine your financial life as a round table you sit at every day. When all five legs are strong in income management, expense control, savings and investment, risk and debt management, and protection and planning, you have stability. You can rest, make decisions with confidence, and even invite others to share in the security and peace you've built. But when one leg wobbles, it affects the whole table.

That's why financial wellness is a journey of ongoing adjustment. Like tightening the bolts on a table leg, you check in, strengthen what's weak, and keep moving forward. Balance is the aim, and balance is what brings lasting peace.

Here's a simple way to visualize your current state:

Pillar	Strength (1–5)	Notes/Concerns
Income Management		
Expense Control		
Savings & Investment		
Risk & Debt Management		
Protection and Planning		

Take a moment to rate yourself honestly. Where are you strong? Where do you need support?

Next Steps

In the chapters ahead, we'll explore each pillar more closely. You'll discover practical ways to strengthen them, along with tools that help you see where you are and where you're heading.

Remember, financial wellness is not a one-time achievement; it's a **practice** It's a rhythm you build, a practice you nurture, and a way of living that grows stronger with time. By keeping all the pillars in balance, you're laying down a foundation sturdy enough to carry your goals, your family, and the future you're working toward.

REFLECTION QUESTIONS

The Pillars of Financial Wellness

- Which of the pillars - income, expenses, savings and investment, risk and debt, or protection and planning - feels strongest in my life right now?
- Which pillar needs the most attention, and why?
- How balanced is my "financial table"? Am I leaning too heavily on one leg while neglecting another?
- What small step can I take this week to strengthen a weaker pillar?
- If I imagine my financial wellness five years from now, which pillar do I most want to see transformed?

Exercise:

Using the worksheet found within this chapter, rate yourself (1 to 5) on each pillar: Income Management, Expense Control, Savings and Investment, Risk and Debt Management.

CHAPTER 4

Measuring Your Financial Wellness

We have established that financial wellness is a state of being, which means it is something we can measure. Just as you might step on a scale, check your pulse, or take a fitness test to understand your physical health, you can use simple, practical tools to assess your financial health. This isn't about complex formulas, endless spreadsheets or intimidating financial jargon; it's about honesty, consistency and a genuine willingness to grow.

Think of it like setting out on a long walk. If you never check a compass or glance at a map, you won't know if you're moving in the right direction. Measuring your financial health works the same way: it gives you a snapshot of where you are today, a reference point for where you want to go, and the reassurance that your steps are carrying you closer to your goals.

For some, the idea of "measuring money" feels daunting. Maybe you've avoided opening your bank app because you don't want to face the numbers, or you've told yourself that as long as the bills are paid, you're doing fine. But ignoring reality doesn't change it; it only delays progress. By contrast, choosing to measure, even when the results are uncomfortable, is an act of courage. It's the first step toward clarity and confidence.

You might find encouragement in the process: perhaps you're saving more than you realised, or you're closer to clearing debt than you thought. Or you may face some hard truths about overspending or neglecting the future. Either way, the power lies in knowing. Awareness brings the ability to act, and that is where change begins.

Measurement is not there to condemn you. It is there to serve you, like a mirror in the gym that shows both where you are and how far you've come. As author James Clear puts it, *"You do not rise to the level of your goals. You fall to the level of your systems."* Measurement helps you build those systems, daily habits and regular check-ins that carry you forward.

In finances, as in life, measurement is not about perfection. It is about steady progress. Each number you record, each habit you adjust, each honest check-in becomes a stepping stone toward a financial life that sustains your well-being and reflects your values.

Why Measurement Matters

Many people avoid looking at their finances because they are afraid of what they might find. It feels easier to look away than to face uncomfortable numbers. But measurement isn't about judgment; it's about awareness. It's about shining a light so you can see clearly and move forward with confidence.

When you choose to measure your financial wellness, you gain:

- **Clarity** – You know exactly where you stand, instead of guessing or assuming.
- **Direction** – You can see what needs attention and where small changes could make a big difference.
- **Motivation** – You can track progress, celebrate wins, and be encouraged by even the smallest step forward.

Without measurement, financial decisions are often based on feelings or guesswork. With it, they become intentional and strategic. Think of it like checking a compass before setting out on a journey: you may still need to walk the road step by step, but now you know you're headed in the right direction.

Six Key Indicators of Financial Wellness

There are six simple markers you can use to check the health of your financial life. Think of them as vital signs, like checking your pulse or blood pressure. They give you a snapshot of where you are, and they're flexible enough to apply no matter your age, income, or stage of life.

1. Net Worth

Formula:
Net Worth = Total Assets – Total Liabilities

Your net worth is a snapshot of your financial position. It tells you what you truly own after subtracting what you owe. At its heart, net worth is a simple question: *if I sold everything I own and paid off everything I owe, what would be left?*

- **Assets (what you own) might include:**
  - Cash and savings
  - Investments (shares, retirement funds)
  - Property (house, land)
  - Valuables (car, jewellery, electronics)
- **Liabilities (what you owe) include:**
  - Credit card balances
  - Loans (student, car, personal)
  - Mortgage
  - Outstanding bills

Why it matters:

Your net worth is like a snapshot of your financial position. A positive number means you own more than you owe; a negative number means debt outweighs your assets. Tracking this over time shows you if you're moving forward (building wealth) or slipping backward.

2. Savings Rate - How Much You Keep

Your savings rate simply measures how much of what you earn actually stays with you. It answers the question: *am I only earning to spend, or am I building something for the future?*

- To calculate it, look at how much you save each month (this could be money set aside for emergencies, retirement, or a specific goal) and divide it by your total income for the month.
- For example: if you earn R20,000 and save R2 000, your savings rate is 10%.

Formula:

Savings Rate = (Monthly Savings ÷ Monthly Income) × 100

This tells you how much of your income you're setting aside. It includes emergency savings, retirement contributions, and goal-based savings.

Why it matters:

Your savings rate shows how prepared you are for the future. Even a modest percentage adds up over time. A healthy goal is between **10–20%**, but the habit matters more than the number. The earlier and more consistently you save, the stronger your safety net becomes.

Think of it this way: every Rand saved is your future self, saying 'thank you'.

3. Debt-to-Income Ratio (DTI) - How Much Debt You Carry

Your debt-to-income ratio shows how much of your monthly income is already tied up in paying off debt. It's like asking: *how much of my salary is already spoken for before I even start the month?*

- To work it out, add up all your monthly debt repayments (credit cards, personal loans, car finance, store accounts, etc.) and divide that by your total monthly income. Then multiply by 100 to get the percentage.
- For example: if you earn **R15,000** and pay **R4,500** towards debts each month, your DTI is **30%**.

Formula:
DTI = (Monthly Debt Payments ÷ Monthly Income) × 100

This measures how much of your income goes toward debt repayment.

Why it matters:

A lower ratio means you have more room to save, invest, or cover life's surprises. A DTI of under **36%** is usually manageable. Anything much higher signals strain, and you may feel like you're working just to pay creditors. The more of your income tied to debt, the less flexibility and freedom you have in making choices for your future.

As financial author Dave Ramsey says, *"Debt is not a tool; it's a barrier."* Keeping your DTI in check helps you move from financial bondage to financial freedom.

4. Emergency Fund Adequacy/Financial Resilience: Can You Withstand Life's Storms?

Life is unpredictable. Cars break down, jobs are lost, medical bills arrive when we least expect them. Financial resilience is your ability to withstand those shocks without your whole life collapsing. It's not just about having money in the bank; it's about having the flexibility, safeguards and habits that allow you to bend without breaking.

At the heart of resilience is an **emergency fund**. Aim to have at least three to six months' worth of essential expenses saved, enough to cover the basics like housing, food, transport and school fees. This cushion gives you room to breathe when the unexpected happens, so you don't have to rely on high-interest debt or scramble in panic.

But resilience goes further than savings. It also means:

- **Adaptability**: the ability to cut back on non-essentials if needed.
- **Diversified income**: not relying on a single source of money when possible.

- **Protection**: using tools like insurance to shield your family from major risks.

Goal:

Aim to have at least three to six months' worth of essential expenses saved. This means covering the basics such as rent or bond, food, transport, utilities and school fees, so that if something unexpected happens, you won't immediately fall into debt.

Why it matters:

Financial resilience isn't about living in fear of "what if." It's about peace of mind. It means knowing that even if life throws a curveball, you have the strength, flexibility, and preparation to face it. As one financial writer observed, *"An emergency fund is not just money in the bank; it's the freedom to breathe when life feels like it's closing in."*

5. Financial Confidence Score

This is the only "indicator" that doesn't rely on numbers. It's about how you feel. On a scale of 1 to 10, how confident are you in your financial future?

Ask yourself:

- Do I feel in control of my money, or does it control me?
- Could I handle a financial emergency without fear?
- Am I moving steadily towards my goals, or am I just drifting?

Why it matters:

Money is not only about maths; it's emotional. Two people with the same income and savings can feel completely different about their situation. Confidence reflects trust: in your plan, in your habits, and in yourself. It's the quiet assurance that you're moving in the right direction, even if you're not "there" yet.

6. Goals Alignment: Are You Building Toward What Matters?

Numbers can tell you a lot, but they don't tell the whole story. You might have a healthy net worth, strong savings and low debt, but if your money isn't aligned with your values, it can still feel empty. Goals alignment asks a deeper question: *is the way I use money building the life I truly want?*

This is where financial wellness moves from survival to significance. It's about ensuring your spending, saving and investing reflect what matters most to you, whether that's family, education, experiences, giving back or building a legacy.

Ask yourself:

- Are my financial habits moving me closer to the life I envision?
- Do my goals reflect my values, or just what others expect of me?
- If I looked back in ten years, would I be proud of how I used my resources?

Why it matters:

Money is not just a means of survival; it's a tool for meaning. When your goals are aligned with your values, financial decisions feel less like sacrifices and more like investments in your best life. As Stephen Covey wrote, *"The key is not to prioritize what's on your schedule, but to schedule your priorities."*

Your Personal Financial Wellness Tracker

Here's a simple table to help you track your wellness indicators:

Indicator	Your Value	Healthy Range	Notes/Actions Needed
Net Worth		Positive and growing	
Savings Rate (%)		10–20% or higher	
Debt-to-Income Ratio (%)		Below 36%	
Emergency Fund (Months)		3–6 months of expenses	
Financial Confidence Score		7–10	
Goals Alignment: Are You Building Toward What Matters?		Clear goals set, 70 -80% of decisions aligned	

Tracking Over Time

Financial wellness is not a once-off achievement; it's a journey. Just as your health changes with time, so does your financial picture. That's why it's important to revisit these indicators regularly. Try checking them monthly or quarterly. Don't worry if progress feels slow; small, steady steps are often the ones that last. The goal is not perfection but direction. Consistency, over time, creates transformation.

Next Steps

In the chapters ahead, we'll look at each indicator more closely and explore how you can strengthen them. You'll find practical tools to increase your savings, reduce your debt, and grow in confidence.

For now, set aside 30 minutes to fill in your tracker. Be honest with yourself; it's not about getting the "right" answers but about understanding your reality. This is your starting point. And every meaningful journey begins with knowing exactly where you are.

REFLECTION QUESTIONS

Measuring Your Financial Wellness

- Which of these indicators feels like my strongest area right now?
- Which one feels like my greatest challenge?
- How honest have I been with myself about where I stand?
- What small step could I take this week to improve just one indicator?

Exercise:
Using the worksheet found within this chapter, fill in your Financial Wellness Tracker (Net Worth, Savings Rate, DTI, Emergency Fund, Confidence Score).

CHAPTER 5

Know Thyself - Personal Values and Financial Goals

Before you can manage your money wisely, you need to pause and ask yourself why. What's the point of all the effort, the saving, the planning, the working and the tracking, if you're not clear on what you're working toward?

Financial wellness isn't just about numbers; it's about **meaning**. It's about aligning your money with your **values**, your **priorities**, and your **vision for life**.

It isn't just about the size of your bank account; it's about the shape of your life. True freedom comes when your money choices reflect your deepest values, not just external pressures or passing desires. For some, that may mean security for family. For others, it may be the freedom to travel, to give generously, or to pursue meaningful work without fear.

This chapter is about clarity. It's about uncovering what matters most to you, and then letting those values guide your financial decisions. Numbers matter, but meaning matters more. When your goals flow from your values, your financial plan stops feeling like a burden and starts feeling like a roadmap to the life you actually want.

Money Is a Tool, Not a Goal

Many people spend their lives chasing money without ever pausing to ask the deeper question: why? More income, bigger savings and a higher salary can all feel like goals in themselves. But money, on its own, is empty. It's only when you use it that it gains meaning. Money is a tool, not the destination.

Think of money like bricks. Bricks alone don't make a home -they need a design, a purpose, and a builder. In the same way, your money is there to build something greater: a life that reflects your values and hopes.

So ask yourself:

- What kind of life do I want to live - peaceful, adventurous, secure, generous?
- What experiences do I want to create for myself and those I love?
- What kind of legacy do I want to leave behind when I'm gone?

The answers to these questions will do more to shape your financial plan than any spreadsheet. A budget keeps you on track, but your values give you the map. When money serves your vision, it becomes powerful, not as a master but as a servant.

Step 1: Identify Your Core Values

Your values are the principles that shape your life. They influence every choice you make, how you spend your time, how you treat others, and how you handle your money. When your financial decisions reflect your values, you experience a sense of peace and alignment. When they don't, you often feel conflicted or unsettled, even if things look fine on the outside.

For example, someone who deeply values family might find greater satisfaction spending money on a family holiday than upgrading to the latest phone. Someone who values growth may choose to invest in further studies rather than buy a new car. These choices might look different on the surface, but they are guided by what matters most at the heart level.

Here are some examples of core values to consider:

- **Security:** I want to feel safe, prepared, and stable.
- **Freedom:** I want to make choices without being tied down by financial pressure.
- **Family:** I want to support, protect, and enjoy life with my loved ones.
- **Growth:** I want to learn, stretch, and invest in my personal or career development.
- **Generosity**: I want to give back and make a difference in my community.

Exercise:

Write down your top 3–5 values. Don't overthink it. Go with what feels most true to you right now. Then ask yourself:

- *How do my current financial habits reflect these values?*

- *Where am I living in alignment, and where am I drifting away from what matters?*

This exercise isn't about judgment; it's about clarity. When you name your values, you begin to give your money direction and purpose.

> "When your values are clear to you, making decisions becomes easier." – **Roy E. Disney**

Step 2: Define Your Life Goals

Once you've clarified your values, the next step is to give them legs by turning them into goals. Values tell you what matters most, but goals give your money direction and purpose. Without them, it's easy to drift, spending and saving without intention.

Think of your goals in layers:

- **Short-term (0–1 year)**: Small, focused wins that build momentum, such as paying off a credit card, saving for a holiday, or setting up a starter emergency fund.
- **Medium-term (1–5 years)**: Milestones that require more planning and consistency, like buying a reliable car, funding further studies, or starting a small business.
- **Long-term (5+ years)**: The bigger dreams that take time and discipline, such as buying a home, preparing for children's education or building a comfortable retirement.

To make your goals more than wishful thinking, you can use **the SMART Framework:**

- **Specific**: Be clear. What exactly do you want?
- **Measurable**: Decide how you'll track progress.
- **Achievable**: Is it realistic with your current resources?
- **Relevant**: Does it connect back to your core values?
- **Time-bound**: Give it a deadline.

Example:
For example, instead of simply saying, *"I want to save money,"* you could say: *"I want to save R10,000 in the next 12 months to enrol in a professional course that will grow my career."*

The difference is clarity. A clear goal directs your energy, shapes your spending, and reminds you why discipline is worth it.

Step 3: Prioritize and Plan

It's normal to have several goals tugging at you at the same time. You may want to pay off debt, build an emergency fund, save for a holiday and invest for retirement all at once. But trying to chase everything at the same time often leads to frustration or burnout. That's why prioritising is so important.

Start by asking yourself:

- *Which goal, if achieved, would reduce my stress the most right now?*
- *Which goal could open up new opportunities for me or my family?*
- *Which goal best supports the bigger vision I have for my life?*

Once you've answered these, rank your goals. Some will need attention immediately (like tackling high-interest debt), while others can wait their turn. This isn't about abandoning dreams; it's about creating focus so you actually get to achieve them.

Then comes the planning. A big goal can feel overwhelming until you break it down. Divide it into monthly, weekly, or even daily action steps. For example, if your goal is to save R12,000 in a year, that's R1,000 per month or roughly R230 per week. Suddenly, the big picture becomes manageable.

Remember: small, steady steps move you further than occasional bursts of effort. Progress doesn't have to be dramatic; it just has to be consistent.

Step 4: Revisit and Revise

Life is never static, and neither are your values or goals. What felt urgent five years ago may not even be on your list today. A new job, a marriage, a child, or even a change in health can shift what matters most. That's why financial wellness isn't about clinging to a rigid plan; it's about staying flexible and realigning as life unfolds.

Think of your goals as a map, not a prison. They guide you, but you're allowed to adjust the route when circumstances change. Build in regular check-ins at least once a year, or whenever you go through a major transition.

Ask yourself honestly: *Are my financial choices still serving my values? Do my goals reflect where I am and where I want to go now?*

By revisiting and revising, you keep your financial plan alive. It grows with you, supports your changing seasons, and always points you back to what matters most.

REFLECTION QUESTIONS

Values and Goals

- What are my top three personal values, the ones that shape how I live and decide?
- Which financial goals truly reflect and support those values?
- What's one small, practical step I can take this week that moves me closer to one of those goals?

WORKSHEET 3

SMART Financial Goals & Values

Align your goals with what matters most.

Value	Goal	Specific	Measurable	Achievable	Time-Bound

CHAPTER 6

Budgeting Without the Boredom

For many people, the word *budget* feels heavy. It brings to mind endless spreadsheets, tight restrictions, and a sense that joy must be sacrificed for discipline. No wonder so many avoid it. But a budget, when seen rightly, is not about cutting happiness out of your life; it's about directing your money so it serves you rather than the other way around.

Think of a budget as a roadmap. Without it, you're driving blind. Money comes in, money goes out, and you're never quite sure where it all went. With it, you have a clear path, a sense of control, and even the freedom to enjoy what matters most to you without guilt.

Budgeting doesn't have to be complicated or boring. In fact, the best budgets are simple, flexible, and personal. They don't box you in; they empower you. When your budget reflects your goals and values, it becomes less about restriction and more about intention. It's not a list of "don'ts," but a guide that says, "This is what matters most to me, and here's how I'll make room for it."

In this chapter, we'll explore practical ways to create a budget that works for you, not against you. You'll learn how to build a plan that reduces stress, honours your priorities, and makes space for joy, all while staying simple, **flexible, and aligned with your goals and values.**

What Is a Budget, Really?

At its core, a budget is simply a spending plan. It's your way of telling your money where to go, instead of scratching your head at the end of the month wondering where it went. A budget is not about saying "no" to everything; it's about making sure you can say "yes" to what matters most.

When done well, a budget becomes less of a restriction and more of a roadmap. It helps you focus on the things that truly add value to your life, while cutting down the noise of unnecessary spending.

A good budget does four things:

- It reflects your priorities, making sure your money supports your goals and values.
- It helps you avoid debt by keeping your spending within healthy limits.
- It builds your savings so you're ready for both opportunities and emergencies.
- It reduces financial anxiety by giving you clarity and control.

As John Maxwell wisely put it, *"A budget is telling your money where to go instead of wondering where it went."*

Think of it less as a cage and more as a compass, something that points you in the direction you want to go.

Step 1: Know Your Numbers

Before you can build a budget that works, you need to get clear on the basics:

1. How much money is coming in each month (after taxes).
2. How much money is going out each month (both fixed and variable).

Fixed expenses are the predictable ones - rent or bond repayments, insurance premiums, loan instalments.

Variable expenses change from month to month - groceries, transport, dining out, entertainment, or even those quick stops for coffee.

Think of this step as turning on the lights in a dark room. Once you can see clearly where your money flows, you can begin to guide it with intention.

Exercise:
Track every cent you spend for one month. You can use a simple notebook, a spreadsheet, or a budgeting app. Categorise each expense, then total it up at the end. Don't judge the numbers, just observe them. Awareness comes before change.

As financial educator Suze Orman once said, *"You can't fix what you don't face."* Getting honest with your numbers is the first act of empowerment.

Step 2: Choose a Budgeting Method

There isn't a single "perfect" way to budget; what works for one person may not work for another. The key is to find a system that fits your lifestyle and helps you stay consistent. Think of it like choosing an exercise routine: some prefer running, others yoga, others the gym. The best method is the one you'll actually stick with.

Here are three tried-and-tested approaches:

1. The 50/30/20 Rule

- **50% Needs:** Rent or bond, food, transport, insurance.
- **30% Wants:** Dining out, hobbies, entertainment, extras.
- **20% Savings & Debt Repayment:** Emergency fund, retirement, paying off loans.
  Best for: Beginners who want a simple, flexible structure that doesn't require tracking every detail.

2. Zero-Based Budgeting

- Every rand is given a job, whether it's for bills, savings, debt or fun.
- Income minus expenses (including savings and giving) equals zero.
  Best for: People who like structure, detail, and knowing exactly where every rand goes.

3. Pay Yourself First

- You decide on a fixed savings amount each month and set it aside first.

- The rest covers expenses and lifestyle spending. Best for: Those focused on building wealth and protecting savings from being "what's left over."

As author John C. Maxwell puts it: *"A budget is telling your money where to go instead of wondering where it went."*

Step 3: Automate and Simplify

Budgeting doesn't have to be complicated or time-consuming. The more you can put on "autopilot," the less you'll need willpower to stay on track. Use tools that take the work out of your hands:

- **Apps:** Try 22seven, Goodbudget, or YNAB (You Need A Budget) to track automatically.
- **Bank alerts:** Set up notifications to let you know when you're close to your spending limits.
- **Spreadsheets:** A simple monthly template with categories can work just as well if you prefer pen-and-paper style tracking.

Automation builds consistency without you needing to think about it every day.

Step 4: Review and Adjust Monthly

Your budget is not carved in stone; it's a living document. Life changes, and your budget should flex with it. Set aside time at the end of each month to:

- Check your progress toward savings or debt goals.

- Adjust for new expenses or changes in income.
- Celebrate wins, no matter how small, and note lessons from slip-ups.

Remember: budgeting is a skill, not a test. Like any skill, you get better with practice.

Step 5: Make Room for Joy

A budget that ignores joy will never last. If you only focus on bills and savings, you'll quickly feel deprived. Include a **"fun fund"** or **"personal joy"** category, money set aside for experiences, hobbies, or simple pleasures. This isn't wasteful; it's part of staying motivated.

TIP: If you overspend one month, don't give up. Adjust and keep moving forward. Progress, not perfection, is what counts.

> "Don't tell me what you value, show me your budget, and I'll tell you what you value." **– Joe Biden**

REFLECTION QUESTIONS

Budgeting Without the Boredom

- Which budgeting method feels most natural to me?
- What are my biggest "spending leaks"?
- How can I make budgeting feel empowering instead of restrictive?

Exercise:

Using the Worksheet provided under Appendix at the back of the book, choose a budgeting method and create a monthly budget.

CHAPTER 7

Income - Your Most Powerful Tool

Income is the engine of your financial life. It's the fuel that powers your budget, savings, investments, and goals. Without it, the other parts of your financial plan, your spending, your saving and your giving, have nothing to run on.

But income is about far more than the number on your payslip. It's not just "how much" you earn, but how you **understand, manage,** and **grow** what flows into your life. For many, income feels like a fixed, unchangeable figure. Yet the truth is that income is dynamic. It can grow, diversify, and evolve as your skills, creativity, and opportunities develop.

Think of income as your most powerful financial tool. A hammer in the wrong hands can cause damage, but used wisely, it builds. Income works the same way: it can be squandered quickly, or it can be harnessed to create stability, opportunity, and long-term wealth.

Step 1: Know Your Income Sources

Before you can plan, you need to be clear on where your money is coming from. Too often, people think only of their primary salary and overlook smaller or less regular streams that also shape their financial picture.

Your income might come from:

- **Primary income:** Salary or wages from your main job.
- **Secondary income:** Freelance work, part-time jobs, overtime pay, commissions.
- **Passive income:** Investments, dividends, rental property income, royalties.
- **Occasional income:** Bonuses, gifts, seasonal jobs, tax refunds, or even selling unused items.

Each of these plays a role. While some are predictable and steady, others may be irregular but still useful. For example, a holiday bonus might not be reliable month-to-month, but it can give you a powerful boost if you plan ahead for how to use it.

Anecdote:

Take L, for instance. She worked full-time as a receptionist and always thought her income was limited to her monthly salary. But when she began tracking, she realised she occasionally earned extra from babysitting, selling baked goods at church, and even from small annual tax refunds. On their own, each stream seemed minor, but when added together, they gave her enough to start an emergency fund she never thought she could afford. Recognising those overlooked sources of income helped her shift from surviving to slowly building stability.

Exercise:

List every possible source of income you have and calculate the average monthly amount. Even if it feels small or irregular, write it down. Seeing the full picture helps you recognise your true earning power. You might be surprised at how much flows through your hands over the course of a year.

Step 2: Growing Your Income

Once you've identified your income sources, the next step is to think about growth. Too often, people only focus on cutting expenses to balance their finances. While reducing costs matters, there's a limit to how much you can cut; there's a ceiling on how much you can save by trimming, but no ceiling on how much you can earn.

Growing your income isn't about chasing wealth for its own sake. It's about creating margin in your life: margin to save, to invest, to give, and to enjoy without the constant shadow of financial pressure.

"Formal education will make you a living; self-education will make you a fortune." — **Jim Rohn**

This reminds us that the journey to increased income often begins with developing ourselves. New skills, new habits, and fresh thinking can unlock opportunities you may never have considered.

How to Grow Your Income:

- **Advance in your current role:** Take initiative, show leadership, or pursue training that positions you for a raise or promotion. Employers value people who solve problems and add measurable value.

- **Explore side hustles:** Freelance, consult, tutor, or sell products and services in your spare time. Many small ventures have grown into thriving businesses.
- **Monetise your hobbies:** A love for photography, writing, baking, or even gardening could bring in extra income when shared with others.
- **Pursue entrepreneurship:** Test a small business idea or monetise a skill online. With consistency, what starts small can grow into a reliable stream.
- **Consider long-term income assets:** Royalties from books, digital courses, or intellectual property. These take effort upfront but create income that flows even when you're not working.

TIP: Investing in yourself through education, mentorship or networking is often the highest-return financial decision you can make.

Anecdote:

K, a schoolteacher, loved woodworking. For years, he only made furniture for himself and friends. But when he decided to list a few pieces online, he was overwhelmed by the demand. What started as a small side hustle grew into a steady income stream that eventually paid off his car loan. K didn't stop teaching, but he discovered that one skill, wisely used, could open a new financial chapter.

Exercise

Write down three ways you could increase your income in the next 12 months.

- One should be immediate (like asking for a raise or extra hours).
- One medium-term (like launching a side hustle).

- One long-term (like building an investment).

Choose one to act on this month. Small, consistent steps build momentum for big results.

Step 3: Diversify Your Income

Relying on a single income source can be risky. A salary may feel stable, but unexpected changes like job loss or illness can unsettle everything. Diversifying your income helps you stay flexible and resilient. Even a small additional stream can strengthen your financial foundation.

As the old proverb says, "Do not put all your eggs in one basket." Spreading your opportunities is one of the simplest ways to protect yourself.

Ideas for diversification:

- Freelance in your field: Use your skills to consult, design, write, or coach.
- Sell products or services online: From handmade crafts to digital downloads.
- Teach or tutor: Share what you know, whether academic, technical, or creative.
- Invest: Dividend-paying shares, property, or collective investments.
- Create digital content: eBooks, courses, podcasts, or creative media.

Anecdote: T, a school secretary, loved baking on weekends. At first, she only made cakes for family events, but a friend encouraged her to advertise locally. Orders began to trickle in, and soon her side business was bringing in R1,500 extra each month. She did not quit her job, but the additional income gave her the freedom to save for emergencies and fund her daughter's school trip without stress. What started small gave her confidence and financial breathing space.

Start small. Even R500 a month from a side activity can add up over time. Diversification is not about replacing your main job immediately but about building resilience step by step.

Exercise

Write down three realistic ways you could diversify your income in the next year. Choose one to explore this month, even if it only brings in a small amount.

Step 4: Manage Irregular Income

Not everyone has a steady monthly salary. Freelancers, small business owners, commission-based workers, and creatives often face income that rises and falls. Some months feel abundant while others are lean. Without a plan, this inconsistency can cause stress and poor financial choices.

The good news is that irregular income does not have to mean instability. With the right systems, you can create consistency and confidence.

Strategies that help:

- **Know your baseline:** Work out the minimum you need for essentials such as housing, food, transport, and utilities.
- **Pay yourself a salary:** In high-income months, avoid overspending. Move the extra into a reserve account and pay yourself a fixed monthly amount.
- **Build a larger buffer**: Salaried workers aim for three to six months of expenses, but irregular earners should aim for six to twelve.
- **Separate business and personal accounts:** Keeping them distinct prevents overspending and keeps your records clear.
- **Plan for taxes:** Set aside a fixed portion of every payment to avoid end-of-year stress.

As financial writer Suze Orman wisely said, "A big part of financial freedom is having your heart and mind free from worry about the what-ifs of life."

For irregular earners, the way to reduce worry is to plan ahead in good months.

Anecdote: C, a freelance graphic designer, used to panic whenever a client delayed payment. Bills piled up, and she often turned to credit cards. Once she began paying herself a set salary and saving more in busy months, her stress decreased. She no longer dreaded quiet seasons because she had created her own safety net.

Exercise

If your income is irregular, calculate your baseline expenses. Commit to paying yourself that amount consistently. In good months, store the extra; in lean months, draw from your reserve. This way, your life stays steady even if your income does not.

Step 5: Earning money is one thing; keeping it and ensuring it continues to flow is another.

Protect and Maximise Your Income

Earning money is one thing; keeping it and ensuring it continues to flow is another. Too many people focus on how much they earn without realising that protecting income is just as important as growing it. One unexpected event, such as illness, retrenchment or even outdated skills, can undo years of progress if you are not prepared.

"Don't work for money. Make money work for you."
– Robert Kiyosaki

This mindset reminds us that income should not only be spent, but stewarded wisely. Protecting it means building resilience against loss, while maximising it means making sure every rand works towards your goals.

Ways to Safeguard Your Income:

- **Insurance cover**: Medical, disability, or income protection policies create a safety net when life throws surprises. Without them, your family's financial stability can collapse overnight.
- **Contracts and agreements**: If you freelance or run a small business, formalise every job. Written agreements reduce the risk of late or unpaid invoices.

- **Tax planning**: Set aside money for taxes in advance. Few things drain progress faster than unexpected tax bills.

Ways to Maximise Your Income:

- **Avoid income leaks**: Cancel unused subscriptions, monitor bank fees, and curb small, unnoticed expenses that drain your wallet each month.
- **Keep your skills current**: The job market changes quickly. Courses, certifications, or simply learning new tools in your field can keep you relevant. Think of skills as income-protecting assets; they hold their value and generate returns.
- **Let money work for you**: Direct part of your income into investments that grow quietly in the background. Even small amounts, consistently invested, build wealth over time.

Anecdote: X had been in IT for years, confident that his role was secure. But when new systems replaced his expertise, he found himself redundant. His colleague M had made it a habit to upskill each year. When the company shifted, she not only kept her job but earned a promotion. M's story shows that protecting income is not just about insurance; it's about preparing for tomorrow by investing in yourself today.

Exercise:
List two actions you can take this month to protect your income (for example, reviewing your insurance or formalising contracts). Then write down one step to maximise it (such as cancelling unused subscriptions, enrolling in a short course, or making a small investment).

Step 6: Align Income with Purpose

At the end of the day, income is only as meaningful as the purpose it serves. More money, on its own, does not guarantee happiness, peace, or fulfilment. What matters is how your income supports your values, your goals, and the life you want to build.

> "Money is a terrible master but an excellent servant."
> – P.T. Barnum

This principle reminds us that money should work for you, not the other way around. Aligning your income with your purpose means asking honest questions:

- Am I earning just to spend, or am I building something that lasts?
- Does the way I use my income reflect my values and priorities?
- Am I creating space to save, invest, and give? Or am I slipping into lifestyle inflation?

Practical ways to align your income with purpose:

- **Pay off debt faster.** Clearing debt creates space for growth, generosity, and peace of mind.
- **Boost savings and investments.** Direct surplus income to strengthen your foundation rather than fuelling short-lived pleasures.

- **Support causes you care about.** Giving transforms income from something personal into something powerful. Even small, regular contributions matter.
- **Invest in meaningful experiences.** Purpose-driven spending might mean prioritising family time, personal growth, or opportunities that enrich your life.

Anecdote: E received a bonus at work and faced a choice: upgrade her car or pay off her last debt. She chose the latter. A year later, she was debt-free, with more monthly breathing room than ever before. Her bonus could have bought status, but instead it bought freedom. Aligning her income with her values gave her lasting peace instead of temporary satisfaction.

Exercise

Take a few minutes to reflect on your income. Write down three ways you could use it more intentionally, whether that's paying off debt, giving more consistently or saving for something that truly matters to you. Then commit to one small step this week to bring your money into closer alignment with your purpose.

REFLECTION QUESTIONS

1. How am I currently using my income, and does it reflect what matters most to me?
2. What small change could I make to use my money more intentionally?
3. Which goal - debt freedom, saving, giving, or investing - would most support my long-term vision?

WORKSHEET 4

Income Sources & Growth Opportunities

List all income streams and how they can grow.

Income Source	Type	Monthly Amount	Growth Opportunity	Next Step

CHAPTER 8

Spending - The Silent Saboteur

Spending is the part of our financial lives that shows up most clearly. You see it in your bank statements, your shopping bags, your bills, and sometimes in the debt that lingers long after the thrill of a purchase has faded. It is also the area where many people feel the least control.

The truth is this: earning more does not automatically solve financial struggles. **How you spend** often matters more than **how much you earn**. Without disciplined and intentional spending, even a higher income can disappear as quickly as it arrives. In fact, history is full of examples of lottery winners, celebrities, and high earners who lost everything because they never mastered the art of managing their outflow.

Spending, left unchecked, is a silent saboteur. It creeps in quietly, disguised as small choices such as the daily coffee run, the "just this once" splurge or the subscription you forgot to cancel, and before long it chips away at savings, undermines goals and creates stress.

But spending can also become a powerful ally. When approached **with awareness, discipline,** and **purpose**, your spending reflects your values and strengthens your financial foundation. Every rand you spend is not just leaving your account; it is casting a vote for the kind of life you are building.

In this chapter, we'll unpack how to recognise unhealthy spending patterns, how to align your expenses with what truly matters, and how to turn your spending into a tool that supports rather than sabotages your financial wellness.

Step 1: Understand Your Spending Habits

Spending is rarely the real problem. More often, the challenge is that we do not actually know where our money is going. Small amounts disappear here and there, like an extra coffee or an unused subscription, until the end of the month arrives and the balance feels far thinner than expected.

The first step toward financial control is awareness. You cannot change what you do not first see clearly. Many people assume they already have a good idea of their spending patterns, yet once they start tracking, they are often surprised at what they discover.

Exercise:
Look back over your last 30 days of transactions using your bank app, card statement, or receipts. Write everything down, then place each item into one of three groups:

- **Needs**: Essentials that keep life stable, such as rent, groceries, utilities, transport, and school fees.

- **Wants**: Extras that bring enjoyment, such as dining out, entertainment, new clothes, or gadgets.
- **Leaks**: Spending that adds no real value, such as unused subscriptions, impulse buys, ATM withdrawal fees, or late payment penalties.

As you sort through your list, notice the patterns. Are your wants overshadowing your needs? Are leaks quietly draining money that could have gone to savings or debt repayment? The results may feel surprising, sometimes encouraging and sometimes uncomfortable, but they are always valuable.

Think of this step like switching on a light in a dark room. The spending has already happened whether you saw it or not. Now, with clarity, you can choose with intention. Awareness transforms spending from something that happens to you into something you direct with purpose.

Step 2: Identify Emotional Spending Triggers

Once you begin tracking your expenses, you may notice that not all spending comes from practical needs. Often, our money choices are less about logic and more about emotion. We buy to feel better after a hard day, to fit in with friends, to celebrate small wins, or simply to break the monotony.

This is what we call emotional spending. It is not always negative. Buying a gift for a loved one or treating yourself occasionally can be healthy and joyful. The danger comes when emotional spending becomes automatic, unplanned, or out of alignment with your values and goals.

Common Triggers to Watch For:

- **Stress or boredom:** Shopping as a distraction or comfort.
- **Peer pressure or social media:** Wanting to keep up with others or copy what you see online.
- **Sales and discounts:** Buying something you did not plan for simply because it feels like a bargain.
- **"I deserve it" thinking:** Using spending as a reward, even when it undermines your financial stability.

TIP: The next time you are about to make a non-essential purchase, pause for a moment. Ask yourself, *"Is this choice moving me closer to my goals, or pulling me further away?"* That single pause can shift you from reacting in the moment to responding with intention.

Step 3: Create a Spending Plan That Reflects You

A good spending plan is not a straightjacket. It is not about saying "no" all the time. Done well, it gives you the freedom to spend on what matters most and to cut back on what does not. Think of it as designing a lifestyle that reflects your values, not just filling in numbers on a page.

Strategies to Shape Your Plan:

- **Try the 50/30/20 rule:** Use half of your income for needs, 30% for wants, and 20% for saving and debt repayment. Adjust the percentages if your situation is different, but let it guide your balance.

- **Set limits for discretionary spending:** For example, decide upfront that you will spend no more than R500 a month on dining out. Clear boundaries protect you from overspending.

- **Use practical tools:** Cash envelopes or prepaid cards can help you manage categories like groceries, entertainment, or transport. When the money is gone, you know it is time to stop.

TIP: Always include a "fun fund." Financial wellness is not only about discipline; it is also about joy. A small allowance for treats, hobbies, or experiences keeps you motivated and makes the plan sustainable.

Step 4: Cut the Leaks and Redirect the Flow

Even the best spending plan can fail if money keeps slipping through unnoticed gaps. These are the small drains such as unused subscriptions, casual impulse buys or bank fees that quietly add up. Left unchecked, they can rob you of hundreds or even thousands each year. The key is not just to spot them, but to redirect that money into areas that actually serve your goals.

How to plug the leaks:

- Review your statements monthly and highlight charges you no longer use or need.

- Cancel subscriptions or memberships that no longer add value.

- Watch out for "small daily habits" like takeaway coffees or repeated delivery fees. Individually, they seem harmless, but over time they snowball.

- Redirect the savings into something purposeful, such as your emergency fund, debt repayments or an investment.

Avoid Lifestyle Inflation

Another hidden leak appears when your income grows but your spending grows just as fast. This "lifestyle inflation" can quietly erode your progress. A new raise, a bonus, or a side hustle payout can feel like an excuse to spend more, but if every increase in income simply funds new expenses, you'll never move forward.

How to stay ahead:

- Increase your savings and investments every time your income grows. Treat it as non-negotiable.
- Keep your core lifestyle simple and intentional, even as you earn more.
- Celebrate income growth with purpose, not impulse, perhaps by funding a long-term goal or investing in something meaningful.

TIP: The secret is to make progress automatic. Each time your salary increases, set up an automatic transfer that raises your savings or investment contribution before you adjust your lifestyle. This way, your future always benefits first.

Step 5: Spend With Intention (Values-Based Spending)

Once you've plugged the leaks and guarded against lifestyle inflation, the next step is to spend with intention. This is where money stops being just a flow in and out of your account, and starts becoming a reflection of who you are and what matters most to you.

Mindful spending means being present in the moment, not just swiping a card out of habit. It means asking yourself questions that anchor your decisions to your values:

- *Do I really need this?*
- *Will this bring lasting value, or just short-term satisfaction?*
- *Is this the best use of my money right now, in light of my goals?*

This doesn't mean never spending on enjoyment. It means choosing joy over impulse, meaning over clutter, and purpose over waste.

TIP: Try delaying non-essential purchases by 24 hours. Most impulse buys lose their shine when you give yourself time to reflect. If you still want it the next day and it fits your values and budget, then go ahead. If not, you've saved yourself money and regret.

Why it matters:

When your spending reflects your values, money becomes more than a transaction; it becomes a tool for peace, freedom and joy. Instead of drifting into debt or clutter, you build a life shaped by conscious choices.

Step 6: Align Spending With Long-Term Goals

Mindful spending shapes today, but alignment ensures your choices build the tomorrow you desire. Every rand you spend is a vote for the kind of life you're creating. The question is: are you casting those votes toward your goals or against them?

When you align spending with long-term goals, you begin to see money not just as fuel for daily life, but as bricks in the foundation of your future.

How to Align:

- **Connect daily spending to future priorities.** Ask: *"Will this choice move me closer to or further from my dream?"*
- **Budget with your goals in mind.** For example, if home ownership is important, trim unnecessary extras and channel more into your house deposit fund.
- **Celebrate progress, not just purchases.** Instead of rewarding yourself with things that set you back, mark milestones with experiences or investments that reflect growth.

Why it matters:

Spending in alignment with your goals transforms money from something fleeting into something lasting. It stops being about quick pleasures and becomes about building a life of meaning, stability, and purpose.

REFLECTION QUESTIONS

Spending: The Silent Saboteur

- When I look at my last 30 days of expenses, what surprised me the most about where my money went?
- Which emotional triggers most often influence my spending, and how can I pause before reacting to them?
- Are there any spending leaks or lifestyle inflation patterns draining my progress? What's one I can cut this month?
- Does my current spending reflect my values, or do I often compromise them for convenience or impulse?
- How can I redirect more of my daily spending toward the long-term goals I care about most?

WORKSHEET 5

Spending Tracker & Leak Detection

Track spending and identify leaks.

Date	Category	Description	Amount	Essential (Y/N)	Notes

CHAPTER 9

Saving: Paying Yourself First

Saving is the cornerstone of financial wellness. It is the quiet discipline that transforms dreams into reality and uncertainty into security. To save is to make a conscious choice: to prioritise your future over immediate impulse, to choose stability over chaos, and to pursue freedom over dependence.

When you save, you are not just setting money aside for "someday." You are actively building a foundation for tomorrow. You are telling yourself and your finances that your goals, your peace of mind and your long-term vision matter. This is why financial experts often say, *"Pay yourself first."* Before creditors, retailers, or unexpected expenses lay claim to your income, you decide to secure a portion for your own growth and future.

But saving is not simply about cutting back or denying yourself joy. It is about being intentional with your money so that it serves you. Even small, regular contributions add up over time. The habit is more important than the amount. A person who saves R500 consistently every month is often in a stronger position than someone who saves R5,000 only once in a while. Consistency creates momentum, and momentum creates results.

At its core, saving gives you options. It provides the breathing space to handle emergencies without panic. It allows you to take advantage of opportunities when they arise. It gives you the freedom to make decisions based on your values, not your fears. And perhaps most importantly, saving is a declaration of self-respect; it is proof that you value your own future enough to prepare for it today.

In this chapter, we will explore how to build a saving habit that is not only consistent but also purposeful. You will learn how to make saving automatic, how to connect it to your personal goals, and how to overcome the common obstacles that often derail good intentions. Saving is not just a financial act; it is a mindset shift. Once you begin to see it as paying yourself first, you will never look at it the same way again.

Step 1: Understand the Purpose of Saving

For many people, saving carries the wrong image. They picture money sitting in an account, untouched, gathering dust, or they associate saving with self-denial, sacrifice or a life of restriction. But true saving is not about hoarding. It is about preparing. It is about choosing security over panic, readiness over regret, and freedom over dependence.

When you save, you are making a statement to yourself: *"My future matters as much as my present."* Saving turns money into more than just numbers on a screen; it becomes a shield against life's surprises and a springboard for life's opportunities. It ensures that when challenges come, you can respond with calm rather than fear. And when opportunities appear, you are ready to step into them without hesitation.

There are three main types of saving, and each plays a unique role in building your financial wellness:

- **Emergency savings.** These are funds reserved for the unexpected. A burst geyser, an unplanned doctor's visit, a broken car, or even the sudden loss of a job can throw your finances into chaos if you are unprepared. Emergency savings protect you from having to rely on debt or scramble for help in those moments.
- **Goal-based savings.** These are savings for the milestones and dreams you want to achieve. Whether it's a family holiday, further education, a wedding, or starting a business, setting money aside with intention keeps your dreams alive. Goal-based saving gives you something to look forward to and transforms aspirations into achievable steps.
- **Long-term savings.** These are funds that shape your future stability and legacy. Retirement, property ownership, and investments for generational wealth all fall here. While they may feel far away, starting early allows compounding and consistency to work in your favour, making the future less of a burden and more of a promise.

Think of saving as building a cushion between you and life's uncertainties. The stronger the cushion, the softer the landing when challenges come. Just as no one would jump without a net, you should not live without savings. That cushion absorbs the shock of hardship and gives you time, space, and confidence to find solutions.

And here is the beauty: saving is not only about protecting yourself from the worst. It is also about positioning yourself for the best. It allows you to say yes to opportunities others might have to decline, whether that's seizing a business idea, enrolling in a course, or taking time off to care for a loved one. Saving is not deprivation; it is empowerment.

Step 2: Make Saving Automatic

One of the biggest challenges people face with saving is not the *desire* to save, but the *discipline*. Good intentions often crumble in the face of daily expenses, unexpected temptations, or the simple thought, *"I'll save what's left at the end of the month."* But here's the truth: very rarely is there anything left at the end of the month. The bills, the wants, and the "just this once" splurges consume it all.

The secret to overcoming this is automation. When you remove the need to decide whether or not to save each month, you also remove the chance of forgetting, delaying, or talking yourself out of it. Saving becomes automatic, predictable, and part of your financial rhythm.

Practical strategies to make saving automatic:

- **Set up an automatic transfer.** Arrange for a portion of your salary to move directly into a savings account the moment it lands in your main account. This way, you never see it as available money to spend; it's already working for your future.

- **Use bank tools that save for you.** Many banks now offer "round-up" features that automatically round your purchases to the nearest rand and send the difference into a savings account. It may seem small, but over time these little amounts quietly accumulate.
- **Treat saving as a bill.** Just as you would never ignore your rent, electricity, or insurance payment, treat saving as a fixed, non-negotiable expense. Write it into your budget as a priority, not an afterthought.

Why this works:

Automation takes saving out of the realm of willpower and makes it a system. You don't need to think about it, and you don't need to wrestle with yourself each month. It just happens. And because it happens consistently, even small amounts grow surprisingly fast.

TIP: Start small if you need to. Even R100 a week adds up to R5,200 a year. It may not feel like much at first, but it's far more than the R0 you'd have if you never started. The power is in the habit. Once the system is in place, you can gradually increase the amounts as your income grows or your confidence builds.

Think of it like planting seeds. Each small, automatic deposit may seem insignificant on its own, but over time those seeds take root, grow, and create a harvest that sustains you.

Step 3: Build an Emergency Fund

If saving is the cornerstone of financial wellness, then your emergency fund is the first wall of protection you build. It's your shield against life's unpredictability, such as the car that breaks down, the sudden medical bill, the unexpected job loss or even the fridge that dies right before payday. Without this safety net, many people turn straight to credit cards, loans, or borrowing from family and friends. An emergency fund keeps you from spiralling into debt when challenges arise.

The goal: Aim to save the equivalent of 3–6 months of essential expenses. If your income is irregular or unpredictable, such as for freelancers, business owners or commission earners, set your sights on 6–12 months. The greater the buffer, the stronger your peace of mind.

Steps to build your emergency fund:

1. **Calculate your essentials.** Write down your basic monthly expenses: housing or rent, groceries, transport, utilities, medical cover, school fees, anything that keeps life stable. This is your baseline number.

2. **Set a target.** Multiply your baseline number by 3–6 (or 6–12 if your income is variable). This gives you a clear savings goal to work toward.

3. **Start small and steady.** Don't be discouraged if the target feels huge. Begin with what you can, whether that's R500, R1,000, or even R100 a month. Progress, not perfection, is what matters.

4. **Keep it separate.** Place this money in a dedicated account, not mixed with your everyday spending. It should be easily accessible in a true emergency, but not so convenient that you're tempted to dip into it for new shoes or a weekend away.

5. **Top it up with extras.** Tax refunds, bonuses, or unexpected income are perfect opportunities to grow your emergency fund faster.

Why this matters:

An emergency fund is not just money in the bank; it is freedom. It allows you to breathe when the unexpected happens. Instead of panicking or scrambling for debt, you can respond calmly, knowing you're prepared. That kind of peace of mind is priceless.

TIP: Guard this fund carefully. It's not for holidays, birthdays, or shopping sprees. Its job is singular and sacred: to be there when you truly need it. If you do use it, make it a priority to replenish it as soon as possible.

Think of your emergency fund like a seatbelt. You hope you'll never need it, but when you do, it can save you from serious harm.

Step 4: Save for Short and Medium Term Goals

While your emergency fund is about security, goal-based saving is about joy and motivation. It's what turns saving from a discipline into something exciting, because instead of simply setting money aside for "someday," you're actively funding the dreams and milestones that matter most to you.

Why it matters:

When you connect saving to something specific and meaningful, the process stops feeling like sacrifice. Each rand saved becomes a step closer to the holiday you've been dreaming of, the laptop that will make your work easier, or the course that will open new doors in your career. This kind of saving fuels both your present motivation and your future satisfaction.

Examples of goal-based savings:

- **R10,000 for a professional course** that boosts your skills and increases your earning potential.
- **R5,000 for a family holiday** that creates memories and strengthens relationships.
- **R20,000 to launch a side business** that diversifies your income and builds future opportunities.
- **R3,000 for a new phone or laptop** to stay efficient and connected.
- **R15,000 for a wedding, anniversary, or special celebration** that honours a life milestone.

Practical strategies for saving toward goals:

1. **Open separate accounts.** Create a dedicated account for each major goal. This way, you can see progress clearly and avoid mixing your holiday savings with your emergency fund.
2. **Name your accounts.** Call them "Italy Trip," "Business Startup," or "New Laptop." A name makes your savings tangible and personal; it's much easier to stay disciplined when you see money piling up under a goal that excites you.
3. **Set timeframes.** Decide when you want to reach each goal. For example: R10,000 in 12 months for a professional course means saving about R833 per month. Breaking it into smaller, manageable steps makes big goals feel possible.
4. **Automate where possible.** If your bank allows, set up recurring transfers into each account. Treat it like paying a bill, but this time the bill is funding your dreams.

5. **Celebrate milestones.** Reaching halfway to your target is an achievement worth recognising. Acknowledge your progress; it keeps you inspired to keep going.

TIP: Mix short-term and medium-term goals. Short-term goals (within 12 months) give you quick wins that keep you motivated. Medium-term goals (1–5 years) help you stay focused and disciplined over a longer journey. Both matter, because they balance immediate satisfaction with future growth.

Remember: Goal-based saving isn't just about money; it's about meaning. It ensures that when you look back at what you've spent your money on, you'll see not just bills and expenses, but milestones, memories, and achievements.

Step 5: Avoid Common Saving Pitfalls

Wanting to save is easy. Following through consistently is where most people stumble. The good news is that many of the obstacles are predictable and preventable. By recognising the common pitfalls, you can plan ahead and stay on track.

1. **Waiting for the "right time."**

It's tempting to think, *"I'll start saving when I earn more"* or *"when things calm down financially."* The reality is, life is rarely free of expenses or unexpected demands. If you wait for the perfect moment, you may never start. The secret is to begin where you are, even if it's just R50 a month. Small beginnings compound into significant progress over time.

2. Saving what's left.

Many people make the mistake of spending first and then saving "if there's anything left." The problem is that there usually isn't. Lifestyle creeps in, and expenses expand to consume whatever is available. Instead, flip the order: treat saving as a non-negotiable bill. Pay yourself first, then spend the rest. This one shift turns saving from an afterthought into a priority.

3. Mixing savings with spending money.

When your savings sit in the same account as your everyday spending, it's far too easy to dip into them, sometimes without even noticing. A separate account creates a psychological barrier. It sends a clear signal: this money is for the future, not for today's impulses. Better still, choose an account that's slightly less convenient to access (like one without a debit card). That extra step discourages unnecessary withdrawals.

4. Ignoring inflation.

The cost of living rises every year. If you save the same amount year after year without adjusting, your savings lose power over time. For example, R1,000 today won't buy the same groceries in ten years. To stay ahead, review your savings goals annually and increase them in line with inflation or salary growth. This ensures that the money you're putting away keeps its real value.

5. Forgetting to set clear goals.

A vague idea like "I should save more" is rarely enough to keep you motivated. Without specific goals, it's easy to lose focus and spend your savings on short-term wants. Clear, tangible targets, whether it's an emergency fund, a holiday or a home deposit, give your savings purpose and make progress visible.

6. **Draining savings for non-emergencies.**

One of the most common pitfalls is dipping into savings for things that aren't true emergencies. A sale at the mall, a last-minute event, or the urge to upgrade your phone might feel urgent, but they don't qualify. Protect your savings by having a small "fun fund" or discretionary budget for those moments, so your long-term goals stay untouched.

Why avoiding these pitfalls matters:

Saving isn't just about putting money aside; it's about creating habits that protect your future. By avoiding these common traps, you ensure that every rand saved moves you closer to security, freedom, and peace of mind.

TIP: Think of saving like planting a tree. If you keep uprooting it or neglecting it, it will never grow strong. But with steady care and patience, it becomes a source of shade, fruit, and stability for years to come.

Step 6: Celebrate Progress and Stay Motivated

Saving can sometimes feel like a marathon with no finish line. You keep putting money aside, but the numbers move slowly, and daily life still demands patience and discipline. That's why celebrating progress is so important. Each milestone, whether big or small, is proof that you are moving closer to financial freedom.

Why celebration matters:

Acknowledging your progress reinforces positive behaviour. It shifts your focus from what you're "giving up" to what you're building. It also keeps you motivated during seasons where saving feels like a grind.

Just like athletes celebrate small victories in training, you can celebrate each step as part of your bigger financial journey.

Ideas for celebrating your savings wins:

- **Track your progress visually.** Use a chart, a tracker app, or even a jar where you drop coloured stones for every R500 saved. Seeing your progress in a tangible way brings your goal to life.
- **Mark milestones with small, meaningful rewards.** This might be treating yourself to a favourite meal, taking a day to rest, or enjoying a low-cost experience with family. The key is to choose celebrations that don't undo your progress.
- **Share your wins.** Tell a supportive friend, family member, or accountability partner when you reach a goal. Sometimes, hearing "well done" is as powerful as the number itself.
- **Connect celebrations to purpose.** Instead of just saying, *"I saved R5,000,"* say, *"I'm now R5,000 closer to my emergency fund, which means more peace and less fear."* This anchors the joy in meaning, not just in numbers.

Avoid the trap:

Be careful not to celebrate progress in ways that sabotage your savings. For example, reaching R10,000 saved and then splurging on a R5,000 gadget defeats the purpose. Celebrations should energise you, not set you back.

TIP: Remember, saving is not punishment. It's not about denying yourself life's pleasures. It is freedom in the making. Each rand saved is like a seed planted—small on its own, but over time it grows into a tree that gives shade, fruit, and stability.

REFLECTION QUESTIONS

- What am I currently saving for, and why does it matter to me?
- How much can I realistically commit to saving each month?
- What small step can I take today to make saving automatic?
- Which of my savings goals excites me the most, and how can I keep that goal visible in my daily life?
- How will I celebrate reaching my next savings milestone?

Exercise:

Using the worksheet provided under Appendix at the back of the book, Set savings goals and automate your savings plan.

CHAPTER 10

Investing - Making Money Work for You

Saving lays the foundation of security. It gives you a cushion against life's uncertainties. But once that safety net is in place, the next step is learning how to grow your money, and that is where investing comes in.

Investing is about putting your money to work so it multiplies over time. Instead of exchanging every rand for hours of labour, you allow your money to become productive on its own. It is the difference between planting a seed and eating it immediately: when you plant it, it grows into a tree that can bear fruit for years to come.

For many people, the word *investing* feels intimidating. It can seem reserved for the wealthy, the experts, or those with complicated spreadsheets. The truth is that anyone can invest, and everyone should. You do not need millions to start. You can begin with small amounts, even a few hundred rand, and grow steadily with discipline and patience.

This chapter will strip away the jargon and fear that often surround investing. You will learn the basics of how investing works, why time is your most powerful ally, and how to choose strategies that align with your goals and your appetite for risk. You will also see why **diversification,** the practice of spreading your money across different assets, is key to reducing risk and increasing long-term growth.

By the end of this chapter, you will not see investing as a mystery or a gamble. You will see it as a practical and accessible tool that can help you build wealth, freedom, and lasting impact.

Step 1: Understand What Investing Is

At its core, investing is about making your money work for you. Instead of simply storing it in a savings account where it sits safely but grows slowly, you put your money into assets that have the potential to grow in value or generate income. Over time, this growth can transform small, consistent investments into significant wealth.

Think of it like planting a tree. When you save, you are putting fruit in a basket and keeping it safe. When you invest, you are planting seeds that can grow into trees which bear fruit season after season. It requires patience, care, and time, but the results are far greater than the single piece of fruit you began with.

Here are some of the most common investment types:

- **Stocks**: When you buy shares, you become a partial owner of a company. If the company grows, your shares increase in value, and you may also receive dividends.
- **Bonds**: Bonds are essentially loans you give to governments or corporations. In return, they promise to pay you back with interest over time.
- **Property**: Real estate can generate rental income or be sold later at a profit. It is often considered a tangible and relatively stable investment.
- **Mutual funds and ETFs**: These allow you to pool your money with other investors. Professionals then manage and diversify the investments, which reduces the risk of putting all your money in one place.
- **Retirement accounts**: These are long-term investment vehicles, often with tax advantages, designed to support you later in life when you no longer earn a salary.

It is important to recognise that investing is not the same as gambling. Gambling is based on chance and short-term speculation. Investing is a disciplined, long-term approach built on informed decisions, diversification, and patience. The goal is not to "get rich quick," but to steadily build wealth and security over time.

TIP: Start with the mindset that investing is a journey, not a single event. You do not need to know everything to begin, and you do not need a large amount of money to take your first step. What matters most is consistency and a willingness to learn along the way.

Step 2: Know Why You're Investing

Before you put a single rand into any investment, pause and ask yourself one key question: *why am I doing this?* Your reason for investing will shape every decision you make, from the type of investments you choose to how long you keep them.

For example, are you investing for **retirement**? If so, your goal is long-term growth, and you can afford to be patient, letting your money ride out the ups and downs of the market. Are you investing for your child's **education**? That is more of a medium-term goal, which means your strategy needs to balance growth with a little more safety. Or are you investing simply to **build wealth** and create opportunities for the future? In that case, your approach might be broader, blending both growth and income-generating options.

Here are three important questions to guide you:

- **What am I investing for?**

  Clarity is power. The clearer your goals, the easier it becomes to choose the right investment vehicles. Retirement, buying property, funding education, or leaving an inheritance are all valid goals, but each one requires a slightly different approach.

- **How long can I leave the money invested?**

  Time is one of the most powerful tools in investing. The longer you leave your money invested, the more it can grow through compounding. But if you know you'll need the money in three years for a deposit on a house, it would not be wise to put it in a high-risk investment that could drop in value in the short term. Matching your time horizon to your investment choice is crucial.

- **How much risk am I comfortable with?**

  Every investment carries some level of risk. Shares can rise and fall dramatically. Property can sit empty between tenants. Bonds are steadier but usually grow more slowly. Knowing your risk tolerance is about understanding yourself. Would you lose sleep if your investments dropped by 10% in a year, or would you stay calm knowing you're in it for the long term? Your answer will shape your mix of investments.

TIP: Write down your goals before you begin. Seeing them on paper makes them real and helps you measure your progress. For example, instead of saying, "I want to invest for retirement," write: "I want to retire at 65 with enough income to cover my monthly needs without relying on others." This gives you a clear target to work toward.

Step 3: Start Small and Stay Consistent

One of the biggest myths about investing is that you need to be wealthy to get started. The truth is, you don't need thousands of rands sitting in your account before you can begin. Many investment platforms today allow you to start with as little as **R100 a month**. The key is not how much you start with, but that you *start.*

Think of investing like planting a tree. If you wait until you can afford to plant a forest, you'll never begin. But if you plant one small tree today and keep watering it, over time it will grow, and soon enough you'll find yourself with a whole garden. Small amounts, consistently invested, grow into something far larger than most people realise.

Here are some beginner-friendly options that make starting simple:

- **Unit Trusts**

These are professionally managed funds where your money is pooled together with other investors. A fund manager spreads it across shares, bonds, and other investments, so you get diversification without having to pick individual investments yourself.

- **Exchange-Traded Funds (ETFs)**

ETFs are another easy entry point. They track the performance of a group of investments, like the top 40 companies on the Johannesburg Stock Exchange (JSE). They are generally low-cost and give you instant diversification.

- **Tax-Free Savings Accounts (TFSAs)**

These accounts are designed to encourage long-term investing. You can invest up to a set limit each year, and the best part is that all your growth, whether from interest, dividends or capital gains, is completely tax-free.

Why consistency matters more than timing:

Many people delay investing because they're waiting for "the right time" to enter the market. But trying to time the market is almost impossible, and even the experts get it wrong. What works far better is consistency. By investing the same amount each month, whether the market is up or down, you take advantage of what's called *rand-cost averaging*. This simply means that sometimes you'll buy at higher prices, sometimes at lower prices, but over time it balances out and smooths your returns.

TIP: Even R100 or R500 a month can grow into a surprising sum over years. Don't underestimate the power of starting small. It's not about waiting until you can invest big; it's about being faithful and steady with what you can manage now.

Step 4: Diversify Your Investments

One of the smartest ways to protect yourself as an investor is to diversify. Diversification means not putting all your money in one place, but spreading it across a range of investments. This way, if one area struggles, the others can help carry you through. It is like planting a garden with different crops: if one fails because of poor weather, the others still grow and provide a harvest.

Diversification is not about avoiding risk altogether, but about making sure that no single setback can derail your entire financial plan. It balances growth and stability so that your investments work together to support your goals.

How to Diversify Wisely

1. **Spread Across Asset Classes**

   The first layer of diversification is across different categories of assets. Stocks, bonds, property, and cash each behave differently. Stocks may grow quickly but can also be volatile. Bonds tend to be steadier, offering lower but more predictable returns. Property can bring long-term growth and rental income, while cash (savings or money market funds) adds stability and liquidity. By combining them, you create balance.

2. **Diversify Within Asset Classes**

Even within one category, it helps to spread your risk:

- **Stocks**: Invest in different industries such as technology, healthcare, retail, energy, and banking. If one industry takes a downturn, others may still perform well.
- **Bonds**: Mix between government bonds (considered safer, with lower returns) and corporate bonds (riskier, but often higher-yielding).
- **Property**: Don't rely on one type. Residential housing, commercial spaces, and property funds such as REITs (Real Estate Investment Trusts) give you variety and reduce dependence on one market.

3. **Use Mutual Funds and ETFs**

For beginners, mutual funds and Exchange-Traded Funds (ETFs) are excellent tools. These are pooled investments that automatically spread your money across dozens or even hundreds of companies or bonds. This gives you instant diversification without needing to pick individual stocks yourself.

4. **Think Local and Global**

Investing only in your home country ties your fortunes to one economy. Adding global investments allows you to benefit from growth in other regions while reducing the impact of local risks such as political instability or currency weakness. A balanced portfolio often has both local familiarity and global reach.

5. **Match to Your Time Horizon**

Different goals call for different mixes of investments.

- For short-term goals (such as saving for a car in two years), you need safer and more liquid options, like bonds or money market funds.

- For long-term goals (such as retirement in 20 years), you can lean toward higher-risk growth assets like stocks or property, since you have time to ride out ups and downs.

6. **Rebalance Regularly**

Markets move, and so will your portfolio. If stocks grow faster than bonds, you might end up with more risk than you originally planned. Rebalancing means adjusting back to your desired mix, usually once or twice a year, so your portfolio reflects your goals rather than market swings.

7. **Avoid Over-Diversification**

Diversification is about strategy, not scattering. Having too many investments can make your portfolio confusing, water down returns, and make it difficult to track progress. Focus on a clear, balanced plan rather than chasing every new product on the market.

Step 5: Understand Risk and Reward

Every investment involves some level of risk. The value of your money can go up, but it can also go down. The art of investing lies in balancing the risk you take with the reward you hope to receive, and matching that balance to your personal goals and timelines.

Think of risk as the bumps in the road, and reward as the destination. A smoother road may feel safer, but it often takes you to a closer, less exciting destination. A rougher road may be harder, but it can lead to greater opportunities if you are willing and able to handle the journey.

The General Rule

- **Short-term goals**: Choose lower-risk investments such as savings accounts, money market funds, or bonds. These preserve your capital and provide stability for goals within the next 1–3 years, such as buying a car or funding a holiday.
- **Medium-term goals**: For goals within 3–7 years, you may include a mix of safer investments and some growth-oriented ones (for example, a blend of bonds and equity funds).
- **Long-term goals**: For goals like retirement, which may be 10, 20, or even 30 years away, you can afford higher-risk investments like stocks or property. Over time, the ups and downs smooth out, and the long-term growth potential is far greater.

Why This Matters

- A young professional saving for retirement in 30 years can take on more risk with stocks because time is on their side.
- A parent saving for their child's university fees in three years should lean toward safer options, since there's little time to recover if the market dips.

Tips for Balancing Risk and Reward

1. **Know your risk tolerance**: Some people sleep soundly through market swings, while others worry at the first dip. Choose investments that align with your comfort level.

2. **Diversify**: A mix of assets helps spread risk. While diversification doesn't eliminate risk entirely, it reduces the impact of any single loss.

3. **Stay informed**: Keep learning about your investments and the markets. Fear often comes from uncertainty, and knowledge builds confidence.

4. **Think long-term**: Short-term volatility is normal. If your goals are far ahead, focus on the bigger picture rather than daily market noise.

Analogy

Imagine planting a tree. If you need shade tomorrow, a fast-growing small plant is better than waiting for an oak. But if you are planting for your grandchildren, the oak, with its slow, steady growth, is worth the wait. The same is true with investing: match the plant to the time and purpose.

Step 6: Avoid Common Mistakes

Even the best investment plan can be derailed by common mistakes. These traps often come from impatience, fear, or lack of knowledge. The good news is that with awareness, you can avoid them and stay on track.

1. Trying to Get Rich Quick

Investing is not a lottery ticket. It is a long-term journey where consistency and patience create wealth. Chasing "get rich quick" schemes often leads to disappointment or, worse, financial loss.

Remember: slow, steady growth is more reliable than promises of overnight riches.

2. Following Hype Instead of Research

Markets are full of noise. Social media, friends, or news headlines may hype up the "next big thing." But what is popular today may collapse tomorrow. Always do your own research and invest in assets that align with your goals and risk tolerance. A sound, boring plan often outperforms a flashy, impulsive one.

3. Ignoring Fees

High management fees, trading costs, or hidden charges can quietly erode your returns over time. For example, a 2% annual fee might not sound like much, but over 20 years it could consume a large portion of your gains. Choose low-cost investment options whenever possible, such as index funds or ETFs.

4. Panicking During Market Dips

Markets naturally rise and fall. A downturn does not mean you've failed; it is part of the process. Many investors lose money not because of the dip itself, but because they panic and sell at the worst time. Instead of reacting emotionally, return to your plan. If your goals are long-term, ride out the storm. Remember, history shows that markets recover over time.

Why This Matters

Avoiding mistakes is just as important as making good choices. Think of investing like climbing a mountain: progress depends not only on moving upward but also on avoiding missteps that could send you tumbling back down.

Step 7: Learn and Grow

Investing is not just about money; it's about building knowledge and confidence. Like any skill, the more you learn, the better your decisions will become. Every investor, even the most successful ones, started as a beginner. The difference between those who succeed and those who stumble is often the willingness to keep learning.

Where to Learn

- **Books**: Timeless guides such as *The Intelligent Investor* by Benjamin Graham (a classic on long-term investing) and *Rich Dad Poor Dad* by Robert Kiyosaki (which explores the mindset of wealth-building).
- **Podcasts**: Accessible learning for your daily commute. Shows like *The Money Show* or *Just One Lap* bring financial conversations into everyday language.
- **Platforms**: South African platforms such as EasyEquities, Satrix, and 22seven offer beginner-friendly tools, educational content, and ways to practise investing without needing large sums of money.

Why It Matters

The investment world changes constantly. New opportunities, new risks, and new tools emerge all the time. By continuing to learn, you stay flexible, informed, and prepared to adjust your strategy as life and markets evolve.

TIP: Start with what you understand. You don't need to know everything before you begin. Focus on one area, whether that's learning about ETFs, understanding how property investing works or simply tracking your first R100 investment. Small, consistent learning builds confidence over time.

Think of this step as sharpening your tools. The sharper they are, the easier it becomes to build something strong and lasting.

Exercise:

Take a few minutes to reflect on your learning journey as an investor. Write down:

- One area of investing you'd like to understand better (e.g., ETFs, property, or retirement funds).
- One resource you will use to learn about it this month (a book, podcast, course, or platform).
- One small action you can take to apply what you've learned (e.g., opening a demo account, making a small test investment, or discussing your findings with a mentor).

REFLECTION QUESTIONS

- Why am I investing, and what specific goals or dreams do I want my investments to support?
- How much can I realistically invest each month, and am I spreading it wisely across different assets?
- How comfortable am I with risk, and does my current approach match my goals and time horizon?
- How can I stay patient and consistent, reminding myself that investing is a marathon, not a sprint?

WORKSHEET 6

Investment Goals & Risk Profile

Define why and how you invest.

Goal	Time Horizon	Risk Level	Expected Outcome

Risk Reflection

How do you respond to market ups and downs?

____

____

____

CHAPTER 11

Debt: Friend or Foe?

Debt is one of the most misunderstood areas of money management. Some people fear it completely, avoiding it at all costs. Others embrace it recklessly, only to find themselves overwhelmed by repayments, fees, and interest. The truth lies somewhere in between: debt can be either a powerful tool or a dangerous burden, depending entirely on how you use it.

For many, debt has opened doors that would otherwise remain closed. A student loan can provide the education that unlocks a career. A mortgage allows a family to own a home rather than rent indefinitely. A small business loan can transform an idea into a thriving enterprise. In these cases, debt acts like a partner, providing leverage to achieve something valuable.

But when misused, debt quickly turns into a foe. Credit cards, payday loans, or "buy now, pay later" schemes can spiral into chains that weigh heavily on your financial life. The stress of mounting bills and rising interest can steal peace of mind and delay your goals for years.

So, is debt your friend or your foe? The answer depends not only on the type of debt but also on your relationship with it. In this chapter, we will unpack the difference between good and bad debt, explore strategies for paying down what you owe, and show you how to approach borrowing with wisdom. With the right mindset and tools, debt can serve you instead of enslaving you.

Step 1: Understand the Types of Debt

Not all debt is the same. Some kinds of debt can move you closer to your goals, while others can quietly pull you further away. The key is to understand the difference between *good debt* and *bad debt*.

Good Debt

Good debt is money you borrow to acquire something that grows in value or increases your earning potential. It is debt that works for you.

- **Examples**: A student loan that leads to a qualification and a higher-paying job, a home loan (mortgage) that allows you to own property, or a business loan that helps you expand a company.
- **Characteristics**: Usually lower interest rates, longer repayment terms, and the potential to increase your wealth or stability over time. Good debt is an investment in your future.

Bad Debt

Bad debt is money you borrow for things that lose value quickly or bring no long-term benefit. It drains rather than builds.

- **Examples**: Credit card debt from impulse shopping, payday loans with extreme interest rates, or store accounts used for clothes, gadgets, or luxuries that don't hold value.
- **Characteristics**: High interest rates, short repayment periods, and no lasting return. Bad debt often leads to a cycle of stress and repayment without progress.

TIP: Before taking on any debt, ask yourself: *"Will this borrowing help me build wealth, security or future opportunities, or am I just funding a short-term desire?"* If the answer is the latter, pause and reconsider.

Step 2: Know Your Debt Numbers

You cannot manage what you do not measure. Many people avoid looking closely at their debt because it feels overwhelming, but clarity is the first step toward control. When you know your numbers, you move from guessing and worrying to planning and acting.

Create a Debt Inventory

Write down every debt you owe. Be specific and honest. For each account, note the following:

- **Type of debt**: Is it a credit card, personal loan, car loan, home loan, or student loan?
- **Outstanding balance**: How much do you still owe in total?

- **Interest rate**: The percentage you're charged for borrowing. Higher rates usually mean higher priority for repayment.
- **Minimum monthly payment**: The least you must pay each month.
- **Due date**: When each payment is expected, to help you avoid late fees and penalties.

This list is your starting point. Keep it somewhere safe and update it regularly.

Calculate Your Debt-to-Income (DTI) Ratio

Your DTI shows how much of your income goes toward paying debt. It is a key measure of whether your debt is manageable or becoming a burden.

The formula is:

$$DTI = \left(\frac{\text{Total Monthly Debt Payments}}{\text{Gross Monthly Income}}\right) \times 100$$

Example

If your total debt payments are R7,200 per month and your gross monthly income is R20,000:

$$DTI = \left(\frac{7,200}{20,000}\right) \times 100 = 36\%$$

A DTI **below 36%** is generally considered healthy. Above that, lenders may see you as risky, and you may feel more financial pressure.

TIP: Think of your DTI as your "financial blood pressure." Just as doctors monitor blood pressure to assess health, monitoring your DTI helps you assess debt health. The lower it is, the more breathing room you have in your finances.

Step 3: Create a Debt Repayment Plan

Once you know your debt numbers, the next step is to create a structured plan for repayment. Without a plan, it's easy to get stuck paying only minimum amounts, which can keep you in debt for years and cost you far more in interest. A repayment plan gives you direction, focus, and hope.

There are two popular approaches to tackling debt:

1. The Debt Snowball Method

- Focus on paying off your **smallest debt first**, regardless of interest rate.
- Continue making minimum payments on all your other debts.
- Once the smallest debt is cleared, take the money you were paying toward it and apply it to the next smallest.
- Repeat until all debts are gone.

Why it works: This method builds **psychological momentum**. Each "quick win" motivates you to keep going. Many people stick to their plan more easily because they see progress fast.

Example: You owe R1,500 on a store card, R8,000 on a personal loan, and R20,000 on a car loan. By paying off the store card first, you get an immediate victory, which energises you to tackle the bigger balances.

2. The Debt Avalanche Method

- Focus on paying off the debt with the **highest interest rate first**, while making minimum payments on all others.
- Once the highest-interest debt is cleared, move on to the next highest.
- This continues until all debts are gone.

Why it works: This method saves you the **most money in the long run** because it reduces the total interest paid.

Example: You owe R5,000 on a credit card at 22% interest, R15,000 on a student loan at 10%, and R100,000 on a home loan at 7%. Even though the credit card balance is smaller than the student loan, the avalanche method tells you to pay it off first because the interest is much higher.

Which Method Should You Choose?

There's no single right answer. The best method is the one you can stick to. If you need quick wins to stay motivated, go with the **snowball method**. If you're more numbers-driven and patient, the **avalanche method** might suit you better.

TIP: Don't worry about being perfect; worry about being consistent. Every extra rand you put toward debt repayment shortens your journey and brings freedom closer.

Step 4: Avoid the Debt Traps

Debt itself is not always the enemy; it is how you manage it that matters. Many people fall into patterns that seem harmless at first but eventually create a heavy financial burden. Recognising these traps early can help you steer clear of them and keep your finances healthy.

Common Debt Traps to Watch Out For:

- Making only minimum payments

It may feel like you're doing the right thing, but minimum payments keep you in debt for much longer and cost you far more in interest. For example, a R5,000 credit card balance with only minimum payments could take years to clear, with interest doubling the cost.

- Impulse borrowing

Loans for things you want but don't need, such as the latest gadget, holiday or night out, create debt without adding lasting value. Over time, this pattern erodes financial freedom and creates regret.

- Ignoring interest rates

Not all debt is equal. A store account at 25% interest grows far faster than a home loan at 10%. If you don't pay attention to these differences, you may end up paying off the wrong debt first or underestimating how fast the balance is growing.

- Using debt to pay debt

Consolidating debt can sometimes help, but borrowing more to cover existing loans is often a dangerous cycle. It creates the illusion of relief but increases the overall burden. This is one of the fastest ways to become trapped in financial stress.

TIP: If you feel overwhelmed or unsure of where to begin, seek guidance from a certified debt counsellor or financial advisor. A fresh, professional perspective can help you create a clear path forward, negotiate with creditors, and rebuild confidence.

Step 5: Use Debt Strategically

Debt is often seen as the enemy, but when handled with wisdom and discipline, it can actually be a powerful tool. The key is to use it for things that add long-term value, rather than for short-term pleasures. Strategic debt builds assets, increases opportunities, and strengthens your future financial position..

Examples of Strategic Debt:

- **Home loans**

  Buying property with a mortgage allows you to build equity over time. Unlike rent, which disappears each month, mortgage repayments contribute toward an asset that usually grows in value.

- **Student loans**

  Education can increase your earning potential for life. While student loans must be approached carefully, investing in a qualification or skill that significantly improves your career prospects can be worth the cost.

- **Business loans**

  Starting or expanding a business often requires capital. A well-planned business loan can create opportunities for growth, new jobs, and wealth generation. The key is to borrow with a clear, realistic plan for repayment.

Questions to Ask Before Taking on Debt:

- *Can I truly afford the repayments?*

  Repayments should fit comfortably into your budget without leaving you stretched or dependent on more borrowing.

- *What is the total cost of the loan?*

  Look beyond the monthly instalments. Factor in interest rates, fees, and the full repayment amount over time. Sometimes a "cheap" loan is far more expensive than it first appears.

- *Is there a better alternative?*

  Could you save up part of the money first, delay the purchase, or explore a lower-cost option? Not every expense requires debt, even when it feels urgent.

TIP: Use debt only when it creates value that lasts longer than the repayment period. If the debt outlives the benefit, such as a high-interest loan for a weekend away, it's a liability, not a strategy.

Step 6: Build a Debt-Free Mindset

Becoming debt-free is more than reaching a number on a statement. It is about reclaiming control over your income, your time and the direction of your life. A debt-free mindset shifts you from constantly looking backwards at what you owe to looking forward at what you can create.

Living without debt doesn't mean you never borrow for strategic reasons (like a home loan or business venture). Instead, it means you refuse to be mastered by debt. You stop using it as a crutch for lifestyle upgrades or quick fixes, and instead build habits of saving, planning, and living within your means.

Practical ways to build a debt-free mindset:

- **Shift your language.** Instead of saying, "I can afford the instalment," start asking, "Can I afford the full cost?" This helps you see the long-term impact of borrowing.
- **Celebrate progress.** Every debt paid off, no matter how small, is a step closer to freedom. Mark these milestones to remind yourself of the bigger picture.
- **Visualise the future.** Imagine your income without repayments dragging it down. What could you save, invest, or experience if every rand you earned was fully yours?
- **Stay accountable.** Share your goals with someone you trust or join a community committed to financial freedom. Accountability strengthens resolve.

Affirmations to adopt:

- *"I control my money; it doesn't control me."*
- *"I use debt as a tool, not a crutch."*
- *"I am building a life of freedom, not obligation."*

TIP: A debt-free mindset is not built in a day; it is strengthened daily through small, consistent decisions. Each time you choose saving over swiping, planning over impulse, or freedom over obligation, you reinforce the belief that financial freedom is not only possible, but inevitable.

REFLECTION QUESTIONS

- What types of debt do I currently hold, and are they helping me build wealth or keeping me stuck?
- What is my Debt-to-Income (DTI) ratio, and what does it reveal about my financial health?
- Which repayment strategy (snowball or avalanche) would keep me most motivated to reduce my debt?
- How would my life change if I were completely debt-free?

Using the worksheet provided under appendix at the back of the book, create a debt inventory and choose a repayment strategy.

CHAPTER 12

Protecting Your Progress

You've worked hard to earn, save, invest, and manage your money. Now comes the part many people overlook: protecting it. Financial wellness is not only about building wealth; it is also about keeping what you've built safe.

Life is unpredictable. A sudden illness, an accident, a legal dispute, or even the loss of a loved one can unravel years of effort if you don't have safeguards in place. Protection is about resilience. It ensures that when storms come, and they will, you don't lose the progress you've made.

Think of your financial journey as building a house. Earning, saving, and investing are like laying bricks and raising walls. Protection is the roof. Without it, everything inside is vulnerable to the elements.

In this chapter, we'll explore practical ways to safeguard your financial life through:

- **Insurance** - protecting against risks you cannot carry alone.
- **Legal planning** - making sure your wishes are honoured and your family is secure.
- **Risk management** - putting strategies in place to reduce vulnerability.

Protecting your progress does not mean living in fear. It means living with peace of mind, knowing that whatever comes, you and your loved ones are prepared.

Step 1: Understand Financial Risk

Financial risk is the possibility that an unexpected event could disrupt your income, increase your expenses, or damage what you've already built. For many people, risk feels like something distant or abstract until it suddenly becomes personal. For many people, risk feels like something distant or abstract until it suddenly becomes personal. A car accident, a hospital bill, or a retrenchment letter can change everything overnight.

The truth is that risk cannot be eliminated completely. Life is uncertain, and no amount of planning can stop challenges from happening. What you can do, however, is prepare for them in a way that limits the financial damage and allows you to recover faster. This is what it means to manage risk wisely.

Some of the most common financial risks include:

- **Illness or injury**: Medical bills can escalate quickly, and time away from work may reduce your income.

- **Job loss or reduced income**: Retrenchments, industry shifts, or even seasonal work changes can leave you vulnerable.
- **Theft or fraud**: With so much banking and shopping now happening online, scams and identity theft are rising threats.
- **Death of a breadwinner**: For families, this can cause sudden financial strain if proper planning isn't in place.
- **Natural disasters**: Fires, floods, or storms can damage property and disrupt your ability to earn.

Each of these risks can feel overwhelming if faced unprepared. Yet with foresight, you can cushion their impact. For example, having health insurance or an emergency fund turns an unexpected hospital bill from a crisis into a manageable setback. A written will or life insurance ensures your family is cared for if the worst should happen.

TIP: Risk is part of life. The key is not to ignore it, but to face it with preparation. You don't need to live in fear of "what if." Instead, create systems such as insurance, savings buffers and legal safeguards that allow you to face those "what ifs" with confidence.

Step 2: Build an Emergency Shield

Your first and most practical line of defence against financial shocks is your **emergency fund**. We introduced this concept in Chapter 9 when talking about saving, but here it takes centre stage as the foundation of protection. Without this shield, even small disruptions such as a car repair, a burst pipe or a week off work due to illness can push you into debt or force you to dip into investments that should have been left to grow.

An emergency fund is not about "if" trouble comes, but **when**. Life is unpredictable, and your emergency fund buys you time, calm, and options. Instead of reacting in panic, you respond with stability because you already have a cushion in place.

How much should you aim for?

- For most people with a regular salary, a fund equal to **3–6 months of essential expenses** is a strong safety net.
- If your income is irregular, seasonal, or commission-based, build a larger buffer of **6–12 months**. This gives you greater peace of mind when income dips.

How to build your emergency shield:

1. **Calculate your essentials.** Work out the bare minimum you need each month for housing, food, utilities, transport, and medical cover. Multiply this by your target months to know your goal.
2. **Start small but steady.** Don't be discouraged if the number feels overwhelming. Even saving R200 a month will grow over time. Progress is more important than perfection.
3. **Keep it separate.** Place your emergency savings in a dedicated account that is easy to access but not too easy to spend. For example, avoid attaching a debit card.
4. **Top it up with extras.** Use bonuses, tax refunds, or side-hustle earnings to build your fund faster.

Why it matters:

An emergency fund is more than money; **it is freedom in the face of uncertainty.** It means you don't have to swipe a credit card in panic, borrow from family, or sell off investments at the worst possible time. It gives you breathing space to make calm, considered decisions instead of desperate ones.

Think of your emergency fund as your personal safety shield. It may not prevent storms from coming, but it will keep you from being swept away when they do.

But some risks are too large for savings alone, which is why insurance is essential.

Step 3: Get the Right Insurance

While your emergency fund protects you against everyday disruptions, there are some risks so large that savings alone cannot cover them. This is where insurance becomes essential. Insurance is essentially a transfer of risk, where you pay a monthly or annual premium so that in the event of a major crisis, the financial weight does not fall entirely on you or your family.

It is not about living in fear of disaster, but about being prepared. Illness, accidents, theft, or loss of life can arrive without warning. Insurance ensures that such events do not wipe out years of progress or leave your loved ones financially vulnerable.

Key types of insurance to consider:

- **Health insurance:** Medical costs can be devastating without cover. Health insurance or medical aid helps you afford treatment, medication, and hospital care without falling into crushing debt.

- **Life insurance:** If you have dependents, life insurance ensures they are financially supported should something happen to you. It provides stability during a time of grief.
- **Disability or income protection insurance:** Your greatest financial asset is not your house or car, it is your ability to earn an income. Disability cover replaces some or all of your income if an illness or injury prevents you from working.
- **Car insurance:** In South Africa, car accidents are common. Insurance is not only a legal requirement for financed vehicles but also protection against the high costs of repairs, theft, or liability.
- **Home or renter's insurance:** Whether you own property or rent, insurance protects your home and possessions against fire, theft, or natural disasters.
- **Funeral cover:** In many cultures, funerals carry significant costs. Funeral cover helps relieve the financial pressure on your family during a difficult time.

Practical tips for using insurance wisely:

1. **Review annually.** The policy you took out five years ago may no longer fit your current responsibilities. Marriage, children, or property ownership often increase the level of cover needed.
2. **Match cover to risk.** If no one depends on your income, life insurance may be less urgent. But if you are a parent or primary earner, it becomes critical.
3. **Avoid over-insurance.** More cover is not always better. Focus on essential policies first, then expand as your budget allows.

4. **Compare providers.** Premiums and benefits vary. Take time to compare policies and ensure you're getting value for your money.

Why it matters:

Insurance acts as a financial safety net for the *big* things that can derail your life. While an emergency fund covers a broken fridge or a few months without work, insurance steps in for medical bills that run into hundreds of thousands, accidents that destroy a car, or the loss of income that would otherwise leave a family destitute. Together, savings and insurance form a dual layer of protection that secures your future and preserves the progress you've already made.

Step 4: Reduce Everyday Risks (Fraud, Theft, Boundaries)

Not all threats to your financial wellness are dramatic. Some creep in quietly, almost unnoticed, through fraud, oversights, or pressure from those around you. Protecting your progress means being vigilant in daily habits and drawing healthy boundaries.

Fraud and identity theft protection

Digital banking and mobile payments make life easier, but they also create new risks. A single compromised password or careless click can undo years of effort. Simple precautions make a big difference:

- Use strong, unique passwords for all financial accounts. Avoid reusing the same one everywhere.
- Enable two-factor authentication wherever possible.

- Check your bank statements and credit reports regularly to catch unusual activity early.
- Never share personal details, like PINs or ID numbers, over email or phone.
- Report suspicious activity immediately to your bank or financial institution. Acting quickly limits the damage.

Protecting your financial boundaries

Not every risk comes from outside. Sometimes, the pressure comes from those closest to us - family, friends, or even business partners. Requests for loans, shared expenses, or unspoken expectations can erode your financial stability if you're not careful. Healthy boundaries keep generosity sustainable.

- Learn to say no when requests exceed your means. Saying no to one request may allow you to say yes to something that truly matters later.
- Keep business and personal finances separate. Mixing the two often leads to confusion, resentment, or even conflict.
- Put agreements in writing, even with friends or relatives. Clear terms prevent misunderstandings and preserve relationships.

TIP: Generosity is noble, but it must be sustainable. If helping others pulls you into debt or jeopardises your own stability, everyone loses. Protecting your progress ensures you're in a position to support others without sinking yourself.

Step 5: Legal and Estate Planning

Protecting your finances isn't only about today; it's also about tomorrow. Legal and estate planning ensures that your hard work and careful choices continue to serve your loved ones long after you are gone or if you are no longer able to make decisions yourself.

Many people think estate planning is only for the wealthy, but it is actually for anyone who wants to leave clear instructions, avoid unnecessary conflict, and ensure their family is provided for. It's not about how much you own, but about taking responsibility for what you do have. Done well, estate planning is one of the most loving and practical gifts you can leave behind.

Essentials to include in your plan:

- **A will.** The foundation of estate planning. It specifies how your assets should be distributed and who will be responsible for carrying out your wishes. Without one, the law decides, which can cause stress and disputes for your family.
- **Beneficiaries.** Keep the beneficiary details on your policies, retirement funds, and savings accounts up to date. Major life changes such as marriage, divorce, or children mean these must be reviewed regularly.
- **Power of attorney.** Appoint someone you trust to manage your financial and legal affairs if you become unable to. This ensures continuity and prevents mismanagement.
- **Living will or healthcare directive.** Clearly outline your preferences for medical care in the event of incapacity. This removes uncertainty for your loved ones at a time when emotions may run high.

TIP: Estate planning is not just a legal formality; it is stewardship. Consult a legal professional to draft or review your documents so they remain valid and relevant. A sound plan ensures your resources are managed with care, your wishes are honoured, and your family is spared unnecessary confusion or hardship.

Estate planning does not just protect your assets; it protects your loved ones from confusion and conflict, ensuring peace at a time when they'll need it most.

Step 6: Review and Update Regularly

Financial protection is not something you set up once and then forget about. Life is dynamic, and as your circumstances change, so should your protection plan. What worked for you five years ago may no longer serve your current needs. A policy taken out before you had children, for example, may fall short of what your family now requires. A will drafted years ago might not include new beneficiaries. Even your emergency fund can become outdated as the cost of living rises.

Major life events such as marriage, the birth of a child, buying property, starting a business, or receiving a promotion are all signals that your financial safeguards need attention. But even without big changes, inflation alone means your safety nets must be reviewed and adjusted over time.

Checklist for Regular Reviews:

- Are my insurance policies still adequate for my current responsibilities?
- Does my emergency fund reflect my present monthly expenses?

- Have I updated my will, beneficiaries, and legal documents recently?
- Are my passwords, online security, and personal financial boundaries still strong?

TIP: Schedule an annual *"financial health check-up."* Just as you visit a doctor for preventive care, make time to review your financial protections before a crisis forces you to. A single day each year spent checking, updating, and adjusting can save you years of regret later.

REFLECTION QUESTIONS

- Which financial risks worry me most right now, and how prepared am I to face them?
- Do I have an emergency fund that truly reflects my current needs and lifestyle?
- Are my insurance policies, estate documents, and digital protections up to date with my present stage of life?
- What regular habits can I adopt to review and strengthen my financial safeguards each year?

WORKSHEET 7

Financial Protection Checklist

Review your protection essentials.

Area	In Place	Details	Action Required
Health Insurance			
Life Insurance			
Disability Cover			
Emergency Fund			
Will / Estate Plan			
Fraud Protection			

CHAPTER 13

Life Happens - Adapting Your Financial Plan

Financial wellness isn't a fixed destination; it's a journey. And like any journey, it comes with detours, surprises, and changes in direction. Whether it's a new job, a growing family, a health challenge, or a global event, life will shift, and your financial plan must shift with it.

This chapter is about building flexibility into your financial strategy so you can adapt with confidence instead of panic. A rigid plan may look neat on paper, but life is rarely that neat. A resilient plan, however, bends without breaking. It allows you to adjust when circumstances change while keeping you on track toward your long-term goals.

Think of it like sailing. You can't control the wind or the waves, but you can adjust your sails. The destination remains the same, but the route may change. Financial resilience works the same way. By learning to adapt, you give yourself permission to keep moving forward even when the path looks different from what you first imagined.

Common life changes that call for financial adjustment include:

- **Career shifts**: A promotion, job loss, or moving into self-employment changes income flow and benefits.
- **Family changes**: Marriage, children, divorce, or caring for ageing parents bring new responsibilities and expenses.
- **Health challenges**: Illness, disability, or increased medical needs affect both income and spending.
- **Economic shifts**: Inflation, interest rate hikes, or global events like pandemics impact everyday costs and investment returns.
- **Life milestones**: Buying a home, starting a business, or planning for retirement require new priorities and strategies.

The key is not to see these as failures of your plan, but as natural parts of life. Your financial plan should be a living document, flexible enough to evolve with you.

TIP: When life changes, don't wait until you're overwhelmed. Pause, review, and adjust your plan. Even small tweaks, such as updating your budget, increasing your insurance or revisiting your savings goals, can make a big difference.

Step 1: Expect Change

Change is one of the few certainties in life. Jobs come and go, families grow and shift, health rises and falls, economies boom and contract. Financial wellness is not about clinging to a perfect plan that never changes, but about recognising that life will bring surprises and preparing yourself to adjust with wisdom.

As the ancient Greek philosopher Heraclitus observed: *"The only constant in life is change."* When you accept this truth, you stop seeing change as a disruption and begin to see it as part of your journey. A job loss can become an opportunity to pivot into a new field. A move to a new city can be a chance to reset your financial habits. Even difficult changes, like illness or divorce, can open the door to new ways of managing resources and building resilience.

Common life changes that call for financial adjustment include:

- **Career transitions**: Starting a first job, shifting careers, promotions, retrenchment, or moving into self-employment.
- **Family milestones**: Marriage, divorce, the birth of a child, or caring for ageing parents.
  Housing moves: Relocating to a new home, buying property, or downsizing for a simpler lifestyle.
- **Health challenges**: Facing illness, injury, or long-term disability that alters both income and expenses.
- **Life seasons**: Retirement, semi-retirement, or pursuing a passion project later in life.

The key is to prepare in advance where possible, but also to build enough flexibility that when surprises arrive, they don't devastate your progress. Having an emergency fund, appropriate insurance, and a clear understanding of your values gives you stability even when circumstances shift.

TIP: Financial wellness doesn't mean you can predict every change. It means you're emotionally and financially ready to adapt. As the proverb says, *"The bamboo that bends is stronger than the oak that resists."* Expect the unexpected, and your plan will bend with the wind rather than break in the storm.

Step 2: Revisit Your Financial Goals Regularly

Your goals should grow as you do. What felt urgent at 25 may feel small at 35, and what once looked distant can become your next right step. Treat your goals as living things that need pruning, watering and, at times, replanting.

As the writer James Clear notes, "You do not rise to the level of your goals. You fall to the level of your systems." A regular review is the simple system that keeps your goals honest and aligned with your real life.

How to run a goal review

1. **Reconnect with your values**

   Read your top three values. Ask: does each major goal still reflect these?

2. **Check relevance**

   For each goal, answer:
   - Is this still important to me?
   - Is this the right timing?
   - Is there a simpler path to the same outcome?

3. **Scale or pivot**

   If a goal feels too big, scale it down into a nearer milestone. If it feels too small, stretch it. If it no longer fits, replace it without guilt. Dropping an outdated goal is progress.

4. **Re-write with clarity**

Update the target amount, deadline and next action. Turn "save more" into "save R1,200 a month for 12 months for a R14,400 home deposit starter."

5. **Triage your top three**

Choose one short term, one medium term and one long term goal to focus on now. Focus beats overwhelm.

6. **Link goals to your budget**

Create or adjust sinking funds so money moves every month toward what matters.

Questions to guide you

- Are my goals still relevant and rooted in my current season of life?
- Do they reflect my values today, not last year's version of me?
- What needs to be scaled up, scaled down or swapped out?

TIP: Set a simple cadence: review goals every 6 to 12 months, and immediately after any major life event such as a job change, move, marriage, divorce or new child. A 30-minute calendar reminder is often the difference between drifting and deliberate progress.

Step 3: Adjust Your Budget and Spending

When life shifts, so do your numbers. A new baby adds nappies, medical visits, and childcare costs. A job promotion may increase income but also tempt you to upgrade your lifestyle without meaning to. Major transitions, whether joyful or challenging, will always echo in your budget.

The wise response is to adjust, not ignore. As the African proverb says, *"When the rhythm of the drum changes, the dance must also change."* Your budget is the dance to life's drumbeat. If you keep moving to an old rhythm, you'll stumble.

Practical ways to adjust your budget and spending:

- **Recalculate your monthly budget.** Write down your current income and expenses, not last year's version. Be honest about what has changed.
- **Identify new or removed expenses.** Maybe you've finished paying off a loan, or perhaps school fees have just begun.
- **Reallocate funds to match priorities.** Shift money from lower-value areas to cover new responsibilities or goals.
- **Anticipate ripple effects.** A move to a new city may not only change rent but also transport costs, grocery prices, or school fees.

TIP: Use budgeting apps, digital trackers, or simple spreadsheets to make adjustments visible and practical. Regular reviews prevent drift and keep your spending aligned with your current reality.

Step 4: Reassess Your Insurance and Protection

As life expands, so do your responsibilities. Insurance that once seemed excessive or unnecessary may suddenly become essential. A young single professional might only need basic health cover, but marriage, children, or buying a home shift the picture dramatically. Protection is not static; it must grow alongside your life.

Areas to review regularly:

- **Health and life insurance.** Ensure you and your loved ones are covered for medical emergencies and, if necessary, supported financially in the event of your passing.
- **Disability and income protection.** Your ability to earn an income is one of your greatest assets. Safeguard it against illness or injury.
- **Home, car, and funeral cover.** As you acquire property or vehicles, or take on family responsibilities, these forms of cover become vital.

Why it matters

Without updating your protection, you may find yourself underinsured just when your family needs support the most. As the saying goes, *"A stitch in time saves nine."* A review today could spare you from deep financial and emotional stress tomorrow.

TIP: Update beneficiaries and coverage amounts whenever your circumstances change, such as marriage, divorce, a new child or the purchase of significant assets. This ensures that your policies always reflect your current reality, not a past season of your life.

Step 5: Update Your Investment Strategy

Just as your life moves through seasons, so should your approach to investing. The strategy that served you well in your twenties may not be the one that fits your forties or retirement years. As your goals, responsibilities, and timelines change, your investment plan must evolve with you.

Examples of shifting strategies:

- **Younger investors** often have the advantage of time. They can afford to take on more risk, such as shares or growth-focused funds, because short-term volatility matters less when the horizon is long.
- **Parents or mid-career earners** may prefer balance. Income-generating assets like bonds or property can provide stability while still allowing for measured growth.
- **Those nearing retirement** usually shift towards preservation. Reducing exposure to riskier assets and focusing on safer, income-based investments can protect what they have built.

Practical steps to adapt your strategy:

- **Rebalance your portfolio.** Over time, market shifts can distort your allocation. Rebalancing helps restore the balance between growth and safety that matches your goals.
- **Adjust contributions.** As your income grows, increase your monthly investment amounts. Even small, steady increases can compound significantly.
- **Explore new options.** Tax-free savings accounts, retirement annuities, or global funds may offer better vehicles depending on your stage of life.

Why it matters

An investment strategy that never changes can leave you overexposed to risk or stuck with limited growth. Adapting ensures your money continues to serve your evolving goals. As the saying goes, *"The wise adapt themselves to circumstances, as water moulds itself to the pitcher."* Flexibility keeps your investments working for you, no matter what life stage you're in.

Step 6: Communicate and Plan with Loved Ones

Money decisions rarely affect only one person. Whether it's a partner, children, or dependents, your financial choices ripple into the lives of those around you. Too often, families avoid these conversations because they feel uncomfortable, but silence can lead to misunderstandings, conflict or even financial hardship when unexpected events arise.

Open, honest communication builds trust and alignment. When everyone understands the goals, priorities, and safety nets in place, the family moves forward as a team rather than individuals pulling in different directions.

Key areas to discuss:

- **Shared goals and responsibilities.** Agree on what matters most, whether that's buying a home, saving for education or preparing for retirement.
- **Budget changes and priorities.** A promotion, job loss, or new baby all affect spending. Keeping everyone in the loop reduces friction.

- **Emergency plans and estate matters.** Talk about what would happen if illness, job loss, or even death occurs. While these topics can feel heavy, they prevent panic and confusion later.

PRACTICAL TIP: Schedule regular "money meetings" with your partner or family. These don't need to be long or formal. Even a monthly conversation over coffee can keep you aligned, celebrate progress, and address challenges before they escalate.

As the African proverb says, *"If you want to go fast, go alone. If you want to go far, go together."* Financial wellness is not just about numbers; it's about unity, shared vision and preparing for the journey as a family.

Step 7: Seek Guidance When Needed

Adapting your financial plan does not mean you have to do everything on your own. Sometimes the wisest step you can take is to reach out for guidance. Just as you would consult a doctor for your health or a mechanic for your car, there are times when financial professionals can save you stress, time, and costly mistakes.

When to seek help:

- **Major financial transitions.** Inheritances, divorce settlements, or receiving a large payout can feel overwhelming. An advisor helps you handle these moments with clarity rather than emotion.

- **Business or property decisions.** Buying, selling, or investing in property or starting a business often involves legal and financial complexity. Professional input protects you from pitfalls.

- **Retirement planning.** Making sure your savings and investments will sustain you for decades requires long-term strategy, not guesswork.

Who to turn to:

- **Financial advisors** for guidance on investments, retirement, or big financial goals.
- **Debt counsellors** if you feel overwhelmed by repayments and need a structured plan.
- **Legal professionals** to help with contracts, estate planning, or disputes.

TIP: Always choose advisors who are qualified, transparent about fees, and aligned with your values. The right advisor empowers you to make informed decisions without pressure.

As the saying goes, *"In the multitude of counsellors there is safety."* Seeking guidance is not a sign of weakness; it's a step of wisdom that can strengthen your financial journey.

REFLECTION QUESTIONS

- What major life changes have I experienced recently, and how have they affected my financial goals or habits?
- When was the last time I reviewed and adjusted my budget, insurance, and investment strategy to reflect my current season of life?
- How often do I communicate with my loved ones about money matters, and what could I do to strengthen those conversations?
- Where could I benefit from outside guidance right now, and who would be the best person or professional to approach?

WORKSHEET 8

Updating Your Financial Plan After a Life Event

Adjust your plan as life changes.

Life Event	Financial Impact	Decisions	Deadline

Checklist

(Found under Appendix at the back of the book)

Life Event Financial Checklist

CHAPTER 14

Teaching and Sharing Financial Wisdom

Financial wellness is personal, but it was never meant to stay private. The lessons you learn, the mistakes you avoid and the wisdom you gain are not just for you; they are seeds that can bear fruit in the lives of others. When you choose to share what you know, you not only strengthen your own habits, you also create ripples of impact that can reach your family, your community, and even generations yet to come.

Money is often a subject shrouded in silence. Families talk about school, careers and even relationships, but too often finances remain unspoken until a crisis forces the conversation. By choosing to break that silence, you become a role model. You show those around you that financial wisdom is not a secret but a skill to be learned, practised and passed on.

Teaching doesn't always mean standing in front of a classroom. It may mean showing your children how to budget their pocket money, guiding a friend through their first investment, or encouraging colleagues to set financial goals. Sometimes, teaching is simply living out good habits so that others see what's possible.

An old African proverb says, *"Wisdom is like fire; people take it from others."* In the same way, your financial wisdom can light a spark in others. When you manage your money well, you create the possibility of shared progress, resilience, and hope.

In this chapter, we'll explore how to step into the role of teacher and mentor, how to pass on financial lessons in a way that inspires rather than lectures, and empowers rather than overwhelms. You'll see how your story, your example and your willingness to share can become tools for transformation, not only for your household but also for your community and the generations that follow.

Step 1: Start with Your Inner Circle

You don't need a classroom, a degree, or a public platform to begin teaching financial wisdom. The most powerful lessons often start at home, in everyday conversations with the people closest to you. Your partner, your children, your siblings, and even your friends form your first circle of influence. How you handle money doesn't just affect you; it shapes their attitudes, their expectations and often their future decisions.

Start by talking openly with your partner about shared goals and money habits. A healthy financial partnership is built on transparency, not secrecy. Create space for conversations about budgeting, saving, and how you'll handle both windfalls and challenges together. These discussions may feel awkward at first, but over time they become a foundation of trust and alignment.

Children are like sponges, and money habits are often formed much earlier than we think. When you teach your child how to save part of their pocket money, delay gratification for something they really want, or give towards a cause, you're not just teaching them about rands and cents; you're shaping their character. They begin to understand discipline, patience, generosity, and responsibility.

Siblings and friends also learn best through shared experiences. Helping a brother understand how to manage debt or showing a friend how you started investing with small amounts may inspire them to take their own first steps. You don't have to have everything figured out; even your mistakes can become powerful lessons. When you share how you overspent, got into debt, or delayed saving, and then explain what you learned, others see both your humanity and your growth.

Practical ideas to try:

- Take your children shopping and let them categorise items into "needs" and "wants." The exercise builds awareness and discernment.
- Discuss the value of work by linking chores or small jobs to pocket money, showing that money is earned, not just given.
- Involve your family in giving decisions, such as choosing a charity together or setting aside a portion of money for community support.

- Be open with siblings or friends about your financial wins and struggles. Let them see that progress is possible, even if it takes time.

TIP: Remember, children and even adults copy more than they listen. A child who sees you swipe a card for every want, or a partner who notices you hide purchases, will pick up habits faster than any lecture can undo. Let your life be the lesson. Practise what you teach, and your inner circle will naturally follow your example.

Step 2: Break the Silence Around Money

In many families and cultures, money is a subject whispered about in private or avoided altogether. Children are told, *"That's not for you to worry about,"* while adults carry the burden in silence. Friends may talk openly about relationships or careers but shy away from finances. This silence often breeds ignorance, shame, and poor decisions. People are left to figure out money through trial and error, sometimes at great cost.

Breaking the silence is one of the most powerful steps you can take toward building financial wisdom, not just for yourself but for those around you. When you bring money into the open, you take away the mystery and the stigma. Conversations about budgeting, debt, saving, and investing become normal, practical, and even empowering.

You don't have to make it complicated. Start with small, honest conversations. Share your own financial journey, your successes, your mistakes and what you've learned along the way. When others see that you are willing to be vulnerable, they feel safer to open up too.

Ways to open conversations:

- Host a monthly "money talk" with your family. Keep it simple: talk about the household budget, saving goals, or how you can cut back on wasteful spending.
- Share a financial book, podcast, or video, then set aside time to discuss what you each learned. Hearing different perspectives makes the lessons more relatable.
- Ask simple but powerful questions, such as: *"What's one thing you wish you had learned about money earlier?"* or *"What financial goal excites you most right now?"*

In friendships, normalise talking about real costs, such as how much rent is, what a loan really means or how to save for travel. Honest dialogue helps others see they are not alone in their struggles or dreams.

TIP: Lead with curiosity, not judgment. Everyone is at a different stage in their financial journey. Your role is not to lecture, but to create a safe space where people feel encouraged to think differently and take action.

Proverb: "He who asks is a fool for five minutes, but he who does not ask remains a fool forever." Talking about money may feel uncomfortable at first, but asking questions and sharing experiences is how wisdom grows.

Step 3: Teach the Basics to the Next Generation

The first classroom for financial literacy is not a school; it's your home. Children and teens absorb money habits long before they ever open a bank account. What they see you doing often speaks louder than anything you say. That's why it is so important to give them the gift of practical financial wisdom early on. These lessons, once learned, can shape their decisions for life. As James Baldwin observed, *"Children have never been very good at listening to their elders, but they have never failed to imitate them."*

Lessons to teach:

- **The difference between needs and wants.** A new toy or the latest shoes may feel urgent, but children should learn to pause and ask: "Do I really need this, or do I just want it?" This simple question builds discernment.

- **The power of saving gradually.** Teach them to put aside small amounts for something they desire instead of expecting instant gratification. Waiting teaches patience and builds a sense of accomplishment when the goal is finally reached.

- **The value of earning.** Whether through chores, creative projects, or small jobs, children learn that money is linked to effort and responsibility. It helps them respect what they earn and spend more wisely.

- **The joy of generosity.** Show them that money is not just for self-consumption. Helping a classmate, contributing to a cause, or setting aside money for giving nurtures compassion and purpose.

Practical tips to make it memorable:

- **Turn it into a game.** Create a "saving challenge" where your child saves for a toy or outing, with a small bonus prize when they reach their goal.

- **Use stories.** Share parables, children's books, or even family experiences that highlight wise and unwise choices with money.
- **Give responsibility.** Allow them to manage a small budget for a family outing, deciding how to spend on food, fun and transport. The experience teaches them trade-offs and accountability in real time.
- **Match their savings.** For every rand or pound they save, contribute a little extra to show the value of discipline and encourage consistency.

Teaching the next generation is about shaping habits and character, not just handling coins and notes. When children see money as a tool for choice, responsibility, and generosity, they are already on their way to a healthier financial future.

Step 4: Lead by Example

The most powerful lessons about money are not taught, they are caught. People, especially children, learn more from what they observe than from what they are told. If you handle money with discipline, generosity, and purpose, you silently teach others to do the same. Your habits set the tone for your household, your friendships, and even your community.

What it looks like in practice:

- **Live within your means.** Resist the temptation to spend more than you earn or to keep up with others. A life of contentment is far more inspiring than one fuelled by debt and comparison.

- **Be consistent in saving and investing.** Small, steady steps speak volumes. Let others see you prioritising long-term growth over short-term pleasures. It shows that building wealth is about discipline, not luck.
- **Demonstrate contentment.** True wealth is not found in constant upgrades or endless consumption. Model the peace that comes from appreciating what you already have, while wisely planning for more.
- **Show generosity.** Involve your family in giving decisions. When children see you give with joy, they learn that money is a tool for impact, not just indulgence.

Proverb: *"The footsteps of the one ahead of you show you the road."* Your example can light a path for those who follow. Long after words are forgotten, the evidence of your financial discipline, peace, and purpose will remain.

Step 5: Share Tools, Not Just Advice

Advice can inspire, but tools empower action. People often know *what* they should do with money, but struggle with *how* to actually do it. By sharing practical resources, you give them something tangible to put into practice right away. As Anton Chekhov once said, *"Knowledge is of no value unless you put it into practice."* Tools turn good intentions into daily habits.

What you can share:

- **Budget templates or apps.** A ready-to-use spreadsheet or a simple app like 22seven or Mint can transform how someone manages their money. Often, people just need a system to follow.

- **Investment platforms you trust.** Show them how you got started. Sometimes the hardest part of investing is opening that first account. Walking someone through a platform removes fear and hesitation.
- **Books, podcasts, or YouTube channels.** Share the content that made financial concepts click for you. A book like *Rich Dad Poor Dad*, a podcast like *The Money Show*, or a video that breaks down investing may be the spark someone else needs.
- **Workshops or community courses.** Encourage participation in local or online financial literacy events. Learning in a group often builds motivation and accountability.

Don't just recommend a tool, offer to walk someone through it. A few minutes of guided support can unlock confidence and momentum. It's like the old proverb: *"Give a man a fish and you feed him for a day. Teach him how to fish and you feed him for a lifetime."* By sharing not just advice but the actual "fishing rod," you empower others to take control of their financial journey.

Step 6: Build Generational Wealth and Wisdom

The greatest gift you can give your family is not only what you leave behind, but also what you pass on while you are alive. Generational wealth is about more than assets; it is about principles, values and knowledge. Money alone can disappear quickly if the next generation does not know how to manage it. Wisdom, however, multiplies as it is shared and lived out. As the old saying goes, *"The wise leave an inheritance, not just of wealth, but of wisdom."*

Ways to build and pass it on:

- **Invest in long-term assets.** Property, retirement funds, or a family business provide stability and opportunities that outlast quick wins.
- **Create a will and estate plan.** This ensures your loved ones are protected and spares them unnecessary conflict during difficult times.
- **Teach financial stewardship.** Show your children and younger family members not only how to save and invest, but also how to handle money with discipline and generosity.
- **Document your journey.** Record your financial story, including both successes and mistakes. These lessons become a map for those who come after you.

Generational wealth is not measured only in rands, pounds, or dollars. It is measured in the security, wisdom, and vision you instil in those who follow. When money and values travel together, they create a legacy that endures far beyond a single lifetime.

Step 7: Be a Financial Wellness Advocate

If you're passionate about financial literacy, don't stop with your own household. Sharing what you've learned with others can spark a ripple effect that transforms families, workplaces, and communities. Knowledge is powerful, but shared knowledge is life-changing.

Ideas to explore:

- **Volunteer in schools or community centres.** Teaching young people the basics of saving, budgeting, or avoiding debt equips them with tools that can shape their future.
- **Use digital platforms.** A blog, podcast, or social media page can reach far beyond your immediate circle, giving practical guidance to people who may never have had access to it otherwise.
- **Host small gatherings.** Workshops, webinars, or informal "money talks" with friends, colleagues, or church groups can create safe spaces for learning and honest conversation.
- **Partner with local organisations.** Community groups, non-profits, or churches often welcome collaboration to spread financial awareness and build healthier habits.

"When you light a lamp for someone else, it also brightens your own path." By sharing what you know, you not only uplift others but also reinforce your own financial discipline and commitment.

TIP: You don't need to be an expert to make a difference. You only need to care, to share, and to be willing to walk with others as they learn. Each story, conversation, and practical tool you pass on has the potential to ignite change far beyond what you can see.

REFLECTION QUESTIONS

Teaching and Sharing Financial Wisdom

- How am I modelling healthy financial habits in my own household, and what lessons are those closest to me learning by watching me?
- Where can I create or encourage safe, honest conversations about money within my family, friendships, or community?
- What practical tools, resources, or experiences can I share that would genuinely help someone take their next step toward financial wellness?
- How can I intentionally pass on both wealth and wisdom, ensuring that my children, dependents or community inherit values as well as resources?

WORKSHEET 9

Financial Literacy Session Plan

Plan a session for your family or community.

Audience	Objective	Topics	Activities	Date

Checklist

Financial Literacy Starter Kit

CHAPTER 15

Your Financial Wellness Blueprint

You've come a long way on this journey. By now, you've discovered the building blocks of financial wellness: how to **earn** and grow your income, how to **spend** with awareness, how to **save** consistently, how to **invest** wisely, and how to **protect** what you've worked so hard to build. You've also explored the importance of adapting to life's changes, aligning your money with your values, and even teaching others along the way.

Now comes the moment to bring all these threads together into a single, practical tool: your **Financial Wellness Blueprint**.

This blueprint is not meant to be a rigid checklist carved in stone. Instead, think of it as a **living, breathing guide,** a framework that evolves as you do. It will help you stay focused on what matters most, measure your progress, and make confident, intentional choices when life presents new opportunities or challenges.

Why a Blueprint Matters

Without a plan, even the best intentions can drift. A blueprint gives you clarity and direction. It allows you to:

- **See the bigger picture** of your financial life at a glance.
- **Stay anchored** to your goals when distractions arise.
- **Adapt with purpose** when circumstances change.
- **Measure progress** and celebrate milestones.

Just as architects use blueprints to guide the construction of a building, your financial blueprint ensures that the "house" of your financial life is built on a solid foundation and grows in line with your design, not by accident.

The Elements of Your Blueprint

A complete financial wellness blueprint weaves together all the areas we've covered so far:

1. **Income Plan** - Knowing your income streams and strategies for growth.
2. **Spending Plan** - Directing your money with intention, cutting leaks, and aligning spending with values.

3. **Savings Strategy** - Building both your emergency shield and your short- and long-term goals.
4. **Investment Roadmap** - Choosing where and how to grow wealth, with diversification and risk balance.
5. **Debt Strategy** - Managing or eliminating debt in a way that serves, not sabotages, your goals.
6. **Protection Plan** - Safeguarding progress with insurance, boundaries, and estate planning.
7. **Adaptability** - Reviewing and adjusting as life changes.
8. **Legacy and Teaching** - Passing on wisdom, not just wealth, to others.

A Flexible Guide

Your blueprint is not about perfection. It's about direction. Life will surprise you with unexpected turns, such as a job change, a new child, a health challenge or even a once-in-a-lifetime opportunity. A good blueprint doesn't crumble under change; it **bends and reshapes** to support you in your new season.

Think of it as a **compass, not a cage**. It points you in the right direction while giving you freedom to adapt your pace and path.

Your Personal Commitment

This blueprint is only as powerful as the commitment behind it. Writing it down makes it real. Reviewing it often keeps it alive. Acting on it consistently transforms it from words on paper into the financial life you desire.

Reflection Exercise: Take some time now to sketch your own Financial Wellness Blueprint.

Break it into the key areas: Income, Spending, Saving, Investing, Debt, Protection, Adaptability, and Legacy. Write down your current reality, your goals, and one step you can take in each area this month.

Over time, these steps will build on one another, creating a life of stability, growth, and purpose.

Step 1: Define Your Financial Wellness Vision

Every strong plan begins with a clear vision. Before you dive into numbers, budgets, or investments, take a step back and ask yourself: *What does financial wellness really mean to me?*

For some, it might mean **security**, the peace of mind that comes from knowing bills are paid and emergencies are covered. For others, it might mean **freedom,** the ability to travel, to work less or to pursue passions without financial strain. For many, it includes **generosity,** being able to give freely to loved ones, causes or communities. And for some, it is about **legacy,** building something lasting for future generations.

Your vision will be as unique as your life, shaped by your values, your dreams, and the season you are in right now.

Questions to guide your vision:

- What does a financially well life look like for me?
- What do I want to feel: secure, free, generous, confident?

- What kind of legacy do I want to leave behind?
- How do I want money to support, rather than control, my choices?

Write your vision statement.

Putting it into words anchors your intentions. Keep it simple but meaningful, something that inspires you when you read it back.

Example: "I want to live a life where I feel secure, can support my family, pursue my passions, and retire with dignity. My finances will give me freedom and peace, not stress or limitation."

TIP: Place your vision statement somewhere visible, such as a journal, a vision board or even a note on your phone. Let it remind you that every rand or pound you manage is shaping the life you desire.

Step 2: Set Your Core Financial Goals

Your financial vision becomes real when you break it into clear, actionable goals. A vision inspires you, but goals guide your daily decisions and give you a roadmap to follow. Without defined goals, it's easy to drift, spending here, saving there, without truly moving toward the future you want.

Think of your goals as the stepping stones between today and your vision of financial wellness. Each step matters, no matter how small.

Break your vision into actionable goals across different timeframes:

Timeframe	Goal Example	Target Date	Monthly Action
Short-term	Save R10,000 for emergency fund	6 months	R1,700/month
Medium-term	Pay off credit card debt	12 months	R1,000/month
Long-term	Invest for retirement	20 years	R2,000/month

Why SMART goals matter:

Make each goal:

- **Specific** – Define the exact outcome (e.g., "Save R10,000," not just "Save more").
- **Measurable** – Track your progress with numbers and milestones.
- **Achievable** – Set targets you can realistically reach given your income and expenses.
- **Relevant** – Ensure each goal connects to your overall vision.
- **Time-bound** – Add deadlines to keep momentum and accountability.

Examples of SMART goals:

- Short-term: "I will save R5,000 in 4 months for a car repair fund by setting aside R1,250 monthly."
- Medium-term: "I will pay off my R12,000 store card within 10 months by paying R1,200 each month."
- Long-term: "I will build a retirement fund of R2 million in 25 years by investing R3,000 monthly."

TIP: Write your top three goals down and review them regularly. Life changes, and so will your priorities. The point is not perfection but direction. Each rand you save, each debt you pay off, and each investment you make is a step closer to your vision.

Step 3: Build Your Financial Dashboard

Just as a car dashboard helps you track speed, fuel, and engine health, a financial dashboard gives you a clear view of your money's "vital signs." Without it, you're driving blind, moving through life without knowing if you're heading toward stability or danger.

Your dashboard doesn't need to be complicated. It's simply a set of indicators you review monthly or quarterly to measure your progress and spot problems before they escalate.

Key Indicators to Track:

Indicator	Current Value	Target Value	Notes/Actions
Net Worth	R25,000	R100,000	Increase savings, reduce debt
Savings Rate (%)	12%	20%	Automate savings
Debt-to-Income Ratio (%)	40%	<36%	Accelerate repayments
Emergency Fund (Months)	2	6	Save R1,500/month
Financial Confidence Score	6	9	Review goals monthly

*Your **Financial Confidence Score** is a self-assessment: How confident do you feel about your financial situation today, on a scale of 1 (very stressed) to 10 (very confident)? Tracking this helps you see how your mindset improves as your numbers improve.

Why this matters:

- **Clarity:** Numbers tell the truth, even when feelings fluctuate.
- **Motivation:** Progress, even in small steps, builds momentum.
- **Course correction:** If an indicator slips (e.g., debt ratio rises), you can act quickly.

Practical tips for setting up your dashboard:

- Use a simple spreadsheet, notebook, or a budgeting app.
- Update it monthly or quarterly. Consistency matters more than perfection.
- Celebrate wins when an indicator moves in the right direction.

TIP: Choose 3–5 indicators that matter most to you. Too many numbers can feel overwhelming, but the right few will give you a powerful snapshot of your financial health.

Step 4: Create Your Monthly Financial Routine

Consistency is what transforms good intentions into lasting results. A financial blueprint is only as strong as the habits that sustain it, and building a steady rhythm ensures you stay aligned with your goals. Think of it as your personal "money fitness plan."

Weekly habits:

- Track your expenses and see where your money is really going.
- Review discretionary spending to spot patterns and keep yourself accountable.

Monthly habits:

- Update your budget to reflect income and expenses.
- Review your financial goals and check your progress.
- Adjust allocations if necessary (for example, moving extra funds into savings or debt repayment).

Quarterly habits:

- Check your net worth to see how your assets and liabilities are shifting.
- Review and rebalance your investments to stay aligned with your risk profile and goals.

Annual habits:

- Review your insurance policies to ensure they still fit your life stage and responsibilities.
- Update your estate plan and beneficiary information.
- Reflect on your financial journey, celebrate progress and identify areas to strengthen.

TIP: Treat these reviews like important appointments. Set calendar reminders, use a digital planner, or tie them to life milestones (e.g., tax season, birthdays, or year-end reflections). Regular check-ins turn financial planning into second nature.

Step 5: Stay Flexible and Reflect Often

Your financial wellness blueprint is not meant to be a rigid contract; it's a living guide that evolves as you do. Life brings change: new jobs, children, health challenges, opportunities and unexpected detours. Flexibility allows you to adapt without losing sight of the bigger picture.

Regular reflection keeps you grounded and intentional. It helps you notice progress, confront challenges honestly, and celebrate wins along the way. Reflection is not about perfection; it's about awareness and growth.

Reflection prompts to guide your review:

- *What worked well this quarter?* (Celebrate habits, decisions, or milestones that moved you forward.)
- *What challenges did I face?* (Identify obstacles, whether emotional, practical or unexpected, that tested your plan.)
- *What adjustments do I need to make?* (Consider shifting budgets, timelines, or strategies to stay aligned with your vision.)
- *What am I proud of?* (Acknowledge even the small wins. Progress builds confidence and momentum.)

TIP: Create a reflection journal or dedicate a section in your planner to these prompts. Looking back over your notes across months or years will give you a powerful picture of growth and remind you how far you've come.

Step 6: Celebrate Your Progress

Financial wellness is not only about numbers; it's about the journey you take and the growth you experience along the way. Every step forward deserves to be recognised. Too often, we focus only on what still lies ahead and forget to pause, reflect, and celebrate how far we've already come.

Celebration doesn't need to be extravagant. It's about marking the moment and reinforcing the positive habits that got you there. When you acknowledge progress, you strengthen your commitment and create the momentum to keep going.

Ways to celebrate your milestones:

- *Paid off a debt?* Treat yourself to something meaningful but modest, such as a dinner out or a new book, without undoing your hard work.
- *Reached a savings goal?* Share the achievement with a friend, partner, or family member. Speaking it out loud makes it feel real and inspires others.
- *Taught someone about money?* Reflect on the ripple effect your actions may have created in their life and future generations.

TIP: Keep a ***financial wins*** journal. Write down each achievement, no matter how small, whether it's sticking to your budget for a month or resisting unnecessary spending. Over time, this record becomes a powerful reminder that progress is possible, even when the journey feels long.

Final Thoughts

You are the financial manager of your life. No one else will care about your money, your dreams, or your future quite the way you do. The good news is that you now have the tools, the mindset, and the plan to steward your finances with confidence.

Whether you are just starting out, rebuilding after setbacks, or fine-tuning what you already have, your financial wellness blueprint is your compass. It will guide your decisions, remind you of your goals, and help you navigate both challenges and opportunities.

Keep learning. Keep adapting. Keep growing. The world around you will change, and so will you, but your commitment to progress will keep you moving forward.

And remember: ***financial wellness isn't about perfection; it's about progress with purpose.*** Every step you take towards clarity, discipline and freedom is a victory worth celebrating.

REFLECTION QUESTIONS

Your Financial Wellness Blueprint

- What does financial wellness truly mean to me, and how does my current lifestyle reflect (or differ from) that vision?
- Which three financial goals are most important for me right now, and how can I make them SMART (Specific, Measurable, Achievable, Relevant, Time-bound)?
- What key indicators (such as savings rate, net worth, or debt-to-income ratio) should I track regularly, and what would progress in those areas look like for me?
- How can I build consistency through a simple financial routine that fits naturally into my weekly, monthly, and yearly life?
- In what ways do I need to stay flexible and adaptable in my plan, and how can I make reflection a regular habit rather than a once-off activity?

WORKSHEET 10

Financial Vision Statement

Write your financial vision below.

My Financial Vision:

DASHBOARD

Monthly Financial Indicators & Routine

Track indicators monthly.

Indicator	Target	Current	Status	Action
Clarity				
Control				
Confidence				
Capacity				
Savings Rate				
Debt Reduction				

APPENDIX

Financial Literacy Starter Kit

Financial wellness is not just about knowledge; it's about practice. This starter kit is designed to give you practical tools, resources, and activities to put what you've learned into action. Use it for yourself, your family, or in group settings.

1. Core Topics to Master

These are the foundations of financial literacy. Start here and revisit them often:

- Budgeting – Create and manage a monthly budget that balances needs, wants, and savings.
- Saving – Build an emergency fund and set goal-based savings targets.
- Debt – Understand good vs bad debt, and use repayment strategies wisely.
- Investing – Learn the basics of compound growth, risk, and diversification.
- Income – Explore ways to earn, grow, and manage multiple income streams.
- Financial Planning – Set SMART (Specific, Measurable, Achievable, Relevant, Time-bound) goals and track your progress.

- Protection – Secure your progress with insurance, fraud prevention, and estate planning.

2. Recommended Tools & Resources

These apps, books, and platforms can help you take the next step:

Apps

- *22seven* – Budgeting and expense tracking
- *EasyEquities* – Beginner-friendly investing platform
- *SatrixNOW* – Access to affordable ETFs and investment products
- *Goodbudget* – Envelope-style budgeting app

Books

- *The Richest Man in Babylon* by George S. Clason
- *Your Money or Your Life* by Vicki Robin
- *I Will Teach You to Be Rich* by Ramit Sethi
- *Money Smart* by Sylvia Walker (South African context)
- *I Wish Someone Had Told Me* by Wendy Selebi (South African context)

Podcasts & Channels

- *The Money Show* with Bruce Whitfield
- *Just One Lap* (South African investing insights)
- *The Dave Ramsey Show* (debt and budgeting strategies)

- Nate O'Brien (YouTube – practical personal finance for young adults)

3. Practical Teaching Activities

These exercises bring money principles to life and work well for individuals, families, or small groups:

- **Budgeting Challenge**

Give yourself (or learners) a mock income and list of expenses. Create a budget using the 50/30/20 rule (50% needs, 30% wants, 20% savings).

- **Savings Goal Planner**

Choose a short-term goal (like R2,000 for a phone). Break it down into weekly or monthly contributions and track progress.

- **Debt Simulation**

Work through a simple loan example to show how interest accumulates over time, and how extra repayments reduce cost and shorten repayment time.

- **Investment Game**

Use a virtual stock market simulator or create a mock investment portfolio. Practise diversifying across shares, bonds, and property, and track growth over time.

4. Printable Templates

(These can be created as worksheets or adapted into apps/spreadsheets.)

- Monthly Budget Worksheet
- Savings Tracker
- Debt Repayment Planner
- Financial Goals Sheet
- Net Worth Calculator
- Emergency Fund Builder

5. Conversation Starters

Use these prompts to open up financial discussions with family, friends, or small groups. Breaking the silence around money builds confidence and shared wisdom:

- "What's one thing you wish you'd learned about money earlier?"
- "How do you decide what's worth spending on?"
- "What's your biggest financial goal right now?"
- "What's your strategy for saving or investing?"

Final Word

This starter kit is not about perfection. It's about progress. Use it as a guide, adapt it to your context, and share it with others. Remember: financial wisdom grows stronger when it is practised and passed on.

Scan the QR Code to get access to your Debt Repayment Planner, Emergency Fund Builder, Financial Goals Sheet, Monthly Budget Template, Net Worth Calculator and Yearly Savings Tracker.

Life Event Financial Checklist

Use this checklist whenever you experience a major life change to stay financially aligned and protected.

Starting a New Job

- ☐ Update your budget to reflect new income
- ☐ Review or start retirement contributions
- ☐ Adjust tax planning and deductions
- ☐ Revisit savings and investment goals

Moving or Relocating

- ☐ Update your budget for new living costs
- ☐ Review or update insurance (home, renter's, car)
- ☐ Plan for moving expenses and deposits
- ☐ Update address with banks and service providers

Getting Married or Partnering

- ☐ Discuss shared financial goals and responsibilities
- ☐ Create or update joint budget
- ☐ Review insurance and beneficiaries
- ☐ Consider a financial agreement (if applicable)

Having a Child

- ☐ Budget for new expenses (childcare, medical, education)
- ☐ Update health and life insurance
- ☐ Start or adjust education savings plan
- ☐ Create or update your will and guardianship plans

Divorce or Separation

- ☐ Separate joint accounts and liabilities
- ☐ Update budget and financial goals
- ☐ Review insurance and estate documents
- ☐ Seek legal and financial advice

Health Crisis or Disability

- ☐ Use emergency fund if needed
- ☐ Review medical aid and disability coverage
- ☐ Adjust budget for treatment or care costs
- ☐ Explore income protection options

Retirement or Career Change

- ☐ Recalculate monthly income and expenses
- ☐ Adjust investment strategy for lower risk
- ☐ Review pension or retirement accounts
- ☐ Plan for healthcare and lifestyle changes

Loss of a Loved One

- ☐ Claim life insurance or benefits
- ☐ Update beneficiaries and estate documents
- ☐ Reassess financial responsibilities
- ☐ Seek emotional and financial support

Take Control. Build Confidence. Create Your Financial Future.

Whether you're just starting your career or navigating the early stages of adult life, *You, the Financial Manager* is your essential guide to mastering money with purpose.

This empowering book redefines financial wellness—not as a distant dream, but as a practical, measurable, and achievable state of being tailored to your unique journey.

Author **Rannoi Sedumo** takes you through fifteen clear and practical chapters that blend financial literacy with personal growth. Along the way, you will discover how to:

- Understand and measure your financial wellness
- Budget without stress or restriction
- Save and invest with clarity and confidence
- Manage debt wisely and protect your progress
- Adapt your financial plan as life evolves
- Share financial wisdom with your family and community

Packed with relatable insights, actionable tools, and a companion workbook, this book will give you the clarity and confidence to become the conscious, capable financial manager of your own life.

Your journey to financial wellness starts here—one decision, one step, one chapter at a time.

www.ingramcontent.com/pod-product-compliance
Lightning Source LLC
LaVergne TN
LVHW100730061126
851857LV00011B/467
* 9 7 8 1 9 9 7 4 6 7 1 8 2 *